Contents

Preface

This fourth edition of Brian Hill's informative book has been updated to take into account recent developments in the European Union including the preparations which are underway for the enlargement of the EU. It has also been expanded by the inclusion of two additional chapters, one on globalisation and one on transition economies.

The publication of this new edition is particularly timely given the increased prominence of the EU in the new A level specifications and degree courses. The book should prove to be especially useful for students preparing for the OCR's Module 2888 Economics in a European Context, AQA's Module 4 Working as an Economist and Edexcel's Unit 6 The UK in a Global Economy.

Susan Grant
Series Editor

Introduction

Why was the Common Market founded? How does it work? Is it a good thing – especially for the UK? What is likely to happen next?

This book presents the facts in an attempt to help its readers to answer these questions. It begins by tracing the origins of the European Economic Community and examining how it has developed into the European Union.

The economic rationale underlying this economic integration is the gains to be obtained from the operation of the *law of comparative advantage* in a free market. But this is a 'text book' theory, so does it really work in the real world? What about imperfections and market failures? In particular what about the infamous Common Agricultural Policy which makes a mockery of the free market concept? Even if the common market does make everyone better off as economic theory suggests, are the gains equitably distributed?

While the current fifteen members are busy deepening the Community why are another dozen clamouring to enter – especially ten central and east European countries suddenly freed by the collapse of communism in 1989?

Twice in this century the larger members of the EU have fought against each other in mutually destructive bloody wars. The human costs are incalculable, the economic costs are small in comparison, yet enormous. The integration of the economies of the fifteen member states has made old enemies into fellow workers and friends; so, by making war amongst its member nations unthinkable the Union must be a great success. But how does its economic performance compare with that of the USA or Japan?

Is the UK better off since joining the EU? Is sovereignty given up or shared as integration proceeds? Should the Union be a looser arrangement of sovereign states benefiting from free trade without the shackles of supra-national policies?

Whilst UK politicians argue, European integration progresses inexorably. Economic and monetary union with a European central bank and a single currency has taken place for twelve EU members. Should the UK adopt the single currency? Will the end of the process be a United States of Europe, and would this be a good, bad or sad thing?

Readers will have to make up their own minds.

The book is divided into 10 chapters. Chapter 1 describes the development of the European Union from the vision of the French economist Jean Monnet through the formation of a customs union, then a common market and now the movement towards economic and monetary union and further enlargement. The chapter also includes an outline of the main EU institutions and the role of the EU budget.

Chapter 2 focuses on the difference between trade blocs and examines the trade creation and trade diversion effects of joining a customs union. In Chapter 3 the ways in which free competition has been, and could be, increased in the EU are explored. Chapter 4 concentrates on the controversial topic of the EU's agricultural policy – the Common Agricultural Policy.

Another major economic policy is the subject of Chapter 5. This is regional policy. The chapter examines why regional variations in income, productivity and employment occur, how regional policy has evolved and why regional policy is likely to become increasingly important in the near future.

The final stage in economic integration, economic and monetary union, is explored in Chapter 6. This is a key issue for the UK with economists and politicians debating the arguments for and against UK membership of the single currency. Chapter 6 discusses these arguments, the process and development of EMU.

Chapter 7 examines the role of the EU in world trade and the impact of globalisation on the EU. In Chapter 8 the progress of two groups of countries, the Commonwealth of Independent States (CIS) and the Central and East European Countries (CEE), making the transition from planned to market economies are compared.

Ten of the CEE countries have applied for membership of the EU. Chapter 9 explores the process and implications of these countries and Cyprus, Malta and possibly Turkey joining the EU.

The final chapter assesses the impact of EU membership on the UK including the effects of the EU's economic strategy, its Common Agricultural Policy and its budget.

Chapter One

Origins of the European Community

'... to establish the foundations of an ever closer union among the European peoples ...' Preamble to the Treaty of Rome

---

What is the European Community, often referred to as 'the Common Market'? It is a combination of fifteen European countries which have decided that their future well-being will be enhanced by their union. They are gradually evolving from independent sovereign states to a federation or 'United States of Europe'. This process of integration is both economic and political. *Whilst this book concentrates upon the economic aspects it must not be forgotten that the fundamental forces involved are political, and so, not surprisingly, are controversial.*

In this chapter the forces which have led to the creation of the Community are outlined briefly and its objectives are analysed against this background. Finally, the Community institutions and the way in which decisions are taken and implemented are examined.

Table 1 overleaf gives some basic data on the size and composition of the Community, and comparative data for the USA and Japan. As the latter two countries are the Community's major competitors they are included in some other tables later in the book.

Historical background

At the conclusion of the Second World War, Europe was devastated economically. It was also fundamentally politically divided into a communist East and a capitalist West. The West included Germany and Italy which, with Japan, had fought on one side in the war, whilst the opposing side, the Allies, had included much of the rest of continental Europe? in addition to Russia, the USA and the British Empire. Soviet Russia and the USA were much larger and more powerful than any other country. Some West European countries feared that their weakened condition constituted a power vacuum which might be too tempting for their huge eastern neighbour. They came together in defence treaties and to cooperate in economic reconstruction.

In the immediate post-war years many economists and politicians produced plans for a better and more secure future. One of the most influential was the French economist **Jean Monnet**. He envisaged a united Europe in which union would bring peace and prosperity to an area where nationalistic division and rivalry had imposed a tradition

Table 1 The European Union in perspective, 1996

	Area (1000 km²)	Population (millions)	GDP (billion Ecus)
Belgium	31	10.2	251.2
Denmark	43	5.3	139.5
Germany	357	82.2	1959.9
Greece	132	10.5	158.1
Spain	505	39.5	726.2
France	544	59.4	1339.3
Ireland	69	3.8	97.1
Italy	301	57.8	1269.5
Luxembourg	3	0.4	17.7
Netherlands	41	15.9	399.0
Austria	84	8.1	199.1
Portugal	92	9.9	167.2
Finland	338	5.2	120.1
Sweden	411	8.9	201.7
United Kingdom	242	59.6	1367.6
EU15 total	3191	376.7	8413.2
USA	9373	273.4	9207.9
Japan	378	127.0	3113.2

Notes: GDPs in terms of purchasing power standards; Germany is the reunified Germany; the order of countries in this and subsequent tables follows European convention, being alphabetical in the native language of each country, e.g. Germany is Deutschland, Spain is Espana, etc.
Source: *European Economy 69.*

of war and misery. He was convinced that a worthwhile future for Europe required economic and political union. The latter had to be a long-term aim since it was unthinkable in the immediate aftermath of bloodshed and bitterness. So he conceived union by degrees, moving gradually from economic cooperation to economic integration, ultimately with full political union as the desired end.

Monnet's vision was given practical expression through the efforts of skilled politicians such as Conrad Adenauer of Germany, Robert Schuman of France and Paul-Henri Spaak of Belgium. *What role did the UK play?* None! The UK emerged from the war as the only major West European country not to be conquered, greatly weakened but still a world power and still possessing an enormous Empire. The latter absorbed British political attention, particularly as the Empire was being turned into a Commonwealth as its members were given sovereignty over their own destinies. So the UK lost the opportunity of playing a leading role in shaping the new Europe.

The reorganised Europe was brought about by the efforts of six countries (**the Six**), these being France, West Germany, Italy, the Netherlands, Belgium and Luxembourg. Working together they created the **European Coal and Steel Community** (ECSC) in 1951, the **European Atomic Energy Community** (Euratom) in 1957, and also in this year signed the **Treaty of Rome**, establishing the **European Economic Community** (EEC) from 1 January 1958. In 1967 these three Communities were merged and the new entity was termed 'the European Community'.

Enlargement of the Community

Although the UK did not relish **economic integration** and the implied loss of sovereignty which this entailed, it did see much sense in cooperation in terms of free trade. Along with other countries having similar attitudes – the traditionally neutral countries – the UK tried to avoid the economic isolation which being outside the EC implied, by forming a free trade area. The **European Free Trade Area** (EFTA) came into being under the **Stockholm Convention**, signed on 4 January 1960. Its signatories were the UK, Austria, Denmark, Norway, Portugal, Sweden and Switzerland; EFTA was confined to trade in manufactures.

By the early 1960s the British government had changed its attitude to the Community. The UK's relative decline as a world power and changing trading patterns convinced British politicians that membership of the Community was desirable. In 1961 Harold Macmillan, the Conservative Prime Minister, announced that the UK would apply to join. This was not a popular move, sentiment being fairly conveyed by the *Daily Mail* cartoon reproduced here. Complicated negotiations followed, but they failed after two years when the French President, General de Gaulle, expressed the opinion that Britain was not yet sufficiently European to be admitted. In a change of government, Labour came to power and in 1967 Prime Minister Harold Wilson announced a new membership application. By the end of the year General de Gaulle had again effectively vetoed UK membership by announcing that such an event would destroy the Community. However, in 1969 he resigned and the Six agreed to open negotiations with the UK, Denmark, Ireland and Norway. The first three subsequently became full members on 1 January 1973. Although Norwegian negotiations also succeeded, the Norwegian people rejected membership in a referendum.

Brig.-Gen. GULLY SQUARE-LEGG, M.C.C.
(President Empire Umpires' Club)

"They'll be wanting us to play French cricket next, dammit!"

Further enlargements added Greece in 1981, Portugal and Spain in 1986. All three countries had emerged from dictatorships immediately before making their applications to join, and saw the Community as offering political stability as well as economic benefits. In 1990, following the collapse of communism in east Europe, East Germany was reunited with West Germany. Finally, Austria, Finland and Sweden joined in 1995. These various enlargements of the Community are a source of confusion to the unwary: obviously Community data refer to a different mix of countries over time. A useful, but unfortunately not universal, convention is to write EUR6, EUR9, EUR10, EUR12 and EUR15. In this book most data relate to EUR15 even for the early years – by the simple expedient of adding figures for the later members to earlier Community data. Mainly resulting from the collapse of communism in east Europe, a further 13 countries have applied to join. Six are expected to accede within five years and the Commission is already referring to EUR21.

Objectives of the European Economic Community

These are best expressed by quoting in full Article 2 of the Treaty of Rome:

'It shall be the aim of the Community, by establishing a Common Market and progressively approximating the economic policies of Member States, to promote throughout the Community a harmonious development of economic activities, a continuous and

balanced expansion, an increased stability, an accelerated raising of the standard of living and closer relations between its Member States.'

This article makes it clear that a common market is expected to be of economic benefit to its members. It ends by looking towards 'closer relations between its Member States', implying that economic progress will lead towards some degree of political integration. This is consistent with the vision of Monnet mentioned earlier.

Although the prime aims of the Community are naturally directed towards its own members, its founding fathers were not entirely inward-looking. Article 110 says that the Community intends to contribute

'. . . *to the harmonious development of world trade, the progressive abolition of restrictions on international exchanges and the lowering of customs barriers'.*

Article 237 says that

'*Any European State may apply to become a member of the Community . . .*'

What is a common market?

The economic principles are to be discussed in the next chapter. For the moment a brief answer is that it is a group of countries which have no trade barriers between its members, but with a common agreed trade policy towards third countries. *Goods, services, labour and capital can circulate freely within and between members as the forces of free competition dictate.* Since one of the main functions of government is to intervene in the national economy, some coordination is essential to prevent the distortion of competitive forces by different government policies operating in the member states. Clearly this coordination requires organising and the Community has special Community level institutions to do this.

Community institutions

There are four major bodies: the European Commission, the Council of Ministers, the European Parliament and the Court of Justice.

The **European Commission** is the civil service of the Community. It is the main initiator of policy proposals, which it drafts and then discusses with the Council of Ministers, Parliament and a variety of interested parties. When policies have been decided it sees to their implementation as **Directives, Decisions and Regulations.** All three types of outcome have the force of law throughout member states – *if* *they conflict with national legislation it is the Community law which must prevail.* **Directives** take effect through national legislatures, which are required to produce their own laws along the prescribed policy lines; that is, the resultant laws are tailored to suit different national circumstances. A **Decision** is binding upon a named person, company or state. **Regulations** are more general, applying in an identical fashion throughout the Community.

When a policy has been agreed by the Council of Ministers, the Commission organises its execution, often with the aid of national civil services. Indeed most of the day-to-day implementation of policies is in the hands of national civil servants acting virtually as agents of the Community – the Commission is too small to do anything more than supervise in this field – far from being the vast 'Brussels bureaucracy' imagined by some nationalists (in fact all of the EU institutions together employ fewer than the number employed by many UK metropolitan borough councils).

The Commission has 20 members appointed by member states, each in charge of a major policy area. The professional civil servants working under them are divided into 26 **Directorates-General** (DGs). These are similar to ministries in the UK. Some of the big ones of immediate interest to economists are DG IV – Competition, DG VI – Agriculture, and DG VII – Transport.

The **Council of Ministers** is not a fixed body of individuals: its composition depends on the policy in question. For example, if the topic is agriculture it is comprised of the Ministers of Agriculture from each member state, for transport policy the Ministers of Transport form the Council. All decisions are taken by the Council of Ministers. They receive proposals from the Commission, they may instruct the Commission to formulate a particular policy, they adopt and amend policies. As the Council is formed of national politicians it is to be expected that much political 'horse trading' takes place which may result in agreements involving unrelated issues despite the best efforts of the Commission.

The **European Council** is a special council of *heads of state or government,* which meets twice a year. This council takes the fundamental decisions of principle, which determine the nature and direction of Community activities. Occasionally the European Council will set up an **Intergovernmental Conference** (IGC) which over a period of months or even years, will look in great detail at a particular policy. For example both the Single European Act and Treaty of European Union (discussed below) were hammered out by IGCs.

8

The **European Parliament** is a directly elected body of 626 members sitting in Strasbourg. It is largely a consultative body, receiving and commenting on Commission proposals before they are adopted by the Council. The latter can pass laws even if the Parliament disagrees with them. However, the Parliament does have some budgetary power and in particular can reject the Community draft budget, which it did in 1985, forcing a new budget to be formulated. It can also, by a two-thirds majority, dismiss the Commission, though it would have no say in the appointment of replacements.

The **Court of Justice** is based in Luxembourg. It has 15 judges, one from each member state. The Court's judgements are binding throughout the Community. Indeed member states or institutions can be taken to the Court by individuals, organisations, other institutions or other member states.

Decision-making and the Single European Act

The Treaty of Rome allowed for decisions to be reached by unanimous agreement during the early years of the Community. Later, with growing political and economic cohesion, decisions were to be reached through a system of qualified majority voting. In practice, member states were very reluctant to give up the power of veto which the unanimity rule implied. Getting the agreement of all member states was never easy and proved increasingly difficult as the Community was enlarged, so that policy initiatives necessary for the development of the Community were only agreed after protracted negotiations. By the early 1980s the Community seemed to be grinding to a halt.

Following much discussion in European Councils and the reports of special committees it was agreed to 'relaunch' the Community via a **Single European Act** (SEA) which was signed by all member states in February 1986. This Act is of great economic and political significance. It amended the Treaty of Rome in an attempt to achieve that Treaty's original economic objective of free trade within the Community. This was to be done by abolishing all internal barriers to trade, producing a **Single Market** by the end of 1992. Achievement of this boost to the Community economy was made possible by dropping the unanimity rule for decisions which did not involve points of principle. Thus decisions in the commercial field were now to be reached by qualified majority voting.

The qualified majority voting system gives ten votes each to France, Italy, Germany and the UK, eight to Spain, five each to Belgium, Greece, the Netherlands and Portugal, four each to Austria and

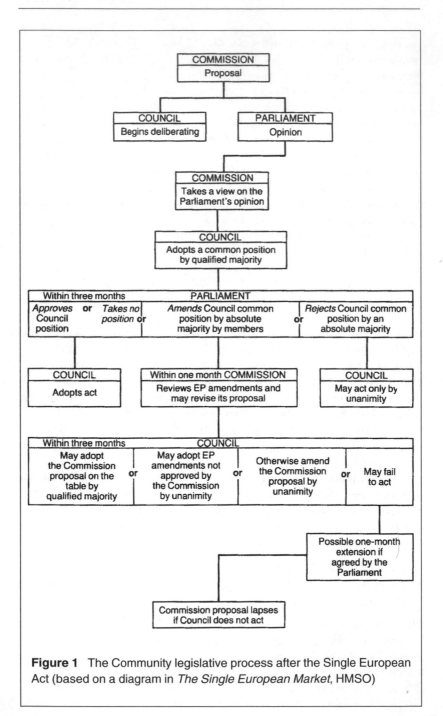

Figure 1 The Community legislative process after the Single European Act (based on a diagram in *The Single European Market*, HMSO)

Sweden, three each to Denmark, Finland and Ireland and two to Luxembourg. The total is 87, and 62 represents a qualified majority. Luxembourg has one vote per 200,000 population, at the other end of the scale the larger countries have one vote for several million people. The system is designed to make it difficult for the larger countries to impose their views on the smaller ones.

The SEA also committed the Community to progress towards **Economic and Monetary Union** (EMU), and politically to include foreign policy and security. In 1989 an IGC was set up to study EMU and make recommendations to the European Council planned for December 1991 in **Maastricht**. Meanwhile the collapse of the USSR power bloc led to the reunification of Germany. This took place in 1990 by East Germany being absorbed into the Community, many were concerned that the enlarged Germany would become introspective and so hinder the further development of the Community. Chancellor Kohl of Germany and President Mitterand of France responded to such worries by proposing that EMU should be accompanied by political union. Accordingly another IGC was set up to examine this, also to report to the European Council in Maastricht in 1991.

The Treaty of Maastricht

This is the popular name given to the **Treaty on European Union** (TEU) which was negotiated in the 1991 European Council. It further amended the Treaty of Rome and so had to be ratified by each of the twelve member states. Sovereignty implications were sufficiently controversial to make ratification by several members a slow and painful process. In the UK, the right wing of the ruling Conservative Party regarded the Treaty as highly undesirable and fought against it. Nevertheless, national ratifications completed, the Treaty was signed in 1992 and came into force on 1 November 1993. Its three main features are:

- economic, social and political extensions to the existing EC
- common foreign and security policy
- intergovernmental cooperation on justice and home affairs.

The latter two aspects are outside the institutional framework of the Community. The net effect of the Treaty is to add a significant political dimension to the EC, the expanded whole forming the **European Union** (EU), this new title will be used in the remainder of this book except in historical contexts.

The Maastricht Treaty provided for a review in 1996 and accordingly another IGC took place in that year resulting in the **Treaty of Amsterdam,** ratified in 1997. This produced minor changes in the functioning of the Community. The Social Protocol for which the UK had agreed an opt out at Maastricht was now brought into the Treaty with UK agreement, it was agreed to give employment a higher priority, and more power to the Parliament. When a new Commission is appointed the member governments agree the new President whose assent is then required for the appointment of each Commissioner and the whole Commission has to be approved by Parliament.

The Treaty of Amsterdam was partly to consider the problems of further enlargements of the EU, but deferred the major decisions to the next IGC. This was to work throughout 2000, concluding in Nice in December. The resulting **Treaty of Nice** reforms the EU institutions ready for the accession of more countries. It has to be ratified by all the member states before coming into force. Its provisions are discussed in chapter 9 in the context of enlargement.

The EU budget

Originally the **EU budget** was designed to be very different from national budgets in that its only purpose was to finance common policies and administration. So it did not involve taxation, borrowing, deficits, or most importantly the redistributive functions of a national budget.

The budget framework was agreed in 1970 and was fully operational by 1975. It then had three sources of income:

- customs duties on imports
- agricultural import levies
- a VAT element.

Under the system of common tariffs, **customs duties** and **levies** are collected at the point of entry regardless of the destination of the imports once within the EU. Thus imports to Germany which arrive at Rotterdam are subject to duty there; clearly it is more reasonable to pay such duties into a common budget than for them to accrue to the member country of the port of origin. Ten per cent of the duties and levies are assumed to be collection costs and are retained by the country of the port of origin.

It should be noted that the **VAT element** is not an EU tax, it only provides a basis for calculating member state contributions to the budget. The Commission calculates the yield which a VAT on a uniform basis would provide if levied in each member country. So this element of the budget relates to a *notional* VAT. In 1970 the maximum rate of VAT was set at 1%.

Budget problems and solutions

In 1984 spending on agriculture increased so much that expenditure seemed certain to exceed revenue. In the event the budget was saved by delaying some payments until the following year and by 'repayable advances' made by member states. The 1984 crisis persuaded the Council of Ministers to agree to curb agricultural spending and to raise the VAT ceiling to 1.4 per cent from 1986. The budget was close to exhaustion in 1986 and 1987. In June 1988 it was agreed to add a fourth source of income (retrospectively from 1 January 1988). This is a **GNP-based contribution** from members. The VAT base was restricted to 55% of GNP immediately but total budgetary expenditure was to be allowed to rise to a maximum of 1.2 per cent of GNP by 1992. A further increase to a maximum of 1.27 per cent of GNP by 1999 was agreed in 1992. In a 1995 'rebalancing' of the budget the VAT base was reduced to 50% of GNP with the rate falling to 1% by 1999. Thus the GNP-based contributions increased whilst the VAT contributions declined – the rebalancing was from VAT which is not related to ability to pay towards GNP-based payments which are. At the same time, the growing importance of the structural funds (see Chapter 5), focused on the poorer member states, means that since 1988 the EU budget has been increasingly undertaking a significant **redistributive role**.

Developments from 2000

With further enlargements imminent, the budget has been modified to emphasise budgetary discipline, each major category of expenditure being subject to strict ceilings, with the total expenditure intended to fall by about 1% by 2006. The overall budget retains its ceiling of 1.27% of GNP for the period 2000-06. This is expected to be sufficient to cover the extra costs resulting from the accession of the six applicant countries expected to join within this period (see Chapter 9 on further enlargement). In a further 'rebalancing' the maximum rate of notional VAT is to be reduced from 1% to 0.75% in 2002 and to 0.5% in 2004. The percentage of customs duties and levies retained by member states as collection costs is increased from 10% to 25%. The correction mechanism for the UK (see Chapter 10) has been retained with minor adjustments.

Table 2 outlines the main elements of the budget for 1999.

Table 2 The EU budget 1999 (million Ecus)

Expenditure		Revenue	
Agricultural price support	40,940	Agricultural levies	1,921
Structural funds	30,659	Customs duties	11,894
Internal polices	4,813	VAT own resources	32,212
External policies	4,298	GNP own resources	37,422
Administration	4,502	Miscellaneous	2,109
Other	346		
Totals	85,558		85,558

Source: *European Economy 69,* 2000.

Conclusion

The UK threw away its post war opportunity to be a major force in the reshaping of Europe. Yet only three years after the Common Market began the UK was applying, unsuccessfully, to join. Subsequently the UK and eight other countries joined, and are now part of a process of increasing integration, the *'ever closer union'* called for in the Treaty of Rome.

KEY WORDS

Jean Monnet	European Parliament
Economic integration	Court of Justice
Political union	Single European Act
Treaty of Rome	Single Market
European Economic	Economic and monetary union
Community	Maastricht
European Community	Treaty on European Union
European Free Trade Area	Treaty of Amsterdam
European Commission	Treaty of Nice
Directives	EU budget
Decisions	Import duties
Regulations	Levies
Directorates-General	VAT element
Council of Ministers	GNP-based contribution
European Council	Redistributive role

The Treaty of Rome

The Treaty of Rome was signed in 1957 and came into force in January 1958. It established Belgium, France, Italy, Luxembourg, the Netherlands and West Germany as a trade bloc, originally called the European Economic Community (EEC).

The Treaty set out the main objectives of the area including balanced economic growth, inter-country co-ordination of economic policy and the creation of a common market.

The objectives of the area's agricultural policy were outlined in Article 39 of the Treaty. These included an increase of agricultural productivity, assured supplies of food, reasonable agricultural prices for the area's consumers and a reasonable standard of living for agricultural workers.

(a) Identify the countries which have joined the European Union since its formation as the EEC in 1958. [2 marks]

(b) Explain what is meant by a common market. [3 marks]

(c) Discuss two benefits of 'inter-country co-ordination of economic policy'. [6 marks]

(d) Outline the details of another Treaty or Act which has amended the Treaty of Rome. [6 marks]

(e) Assess how successful the EU has been in achieving 'reasonable agricultural prices for the area's consumers'. [7 marks]

Chapter Two
Economic integration

'... the principle of comparative advantage ... is perhaps the most powerful idea in economics...' The Economist

This chapter attempts to answer the question – what are the economic benefits of a common market? On the theoretical side the gains from trade, due to the operation of comparative advantage, are analysed and related to different levels of economic integration. Finally, the expected size of gains to be achieved by the EU are discussed. This sets the scene for the remaining chapters which examine the activities of the EU in attempting to achieve these theoretical gains.

The gains from trade

Fundamental to any study of trade is David Ricardo's **Law of Comparative Advantage.** Most readers will be familiar with this law, but a thorough understanding should be ensured by studying Box 2 from *The Economist* of 22 September 1990 (opposite). Briefly, the law states that even if one country is absolutely more efficient in the production of every good than is some second country, if each country specialises in the production of the products in which it has a comparative advantage (i.e. greatest *relative* efficiency – it produces the goods it is *best* at producing), then trade will benefit both countries.

The benefits of trade due to comparative advantage are reinforced by **economies of size** (usually referred to incorrectly as economies of scale). This refers to the fact that, for many forms of production, average costs decline as output is expanded, at least until very large outputs are achieved. Specialisation according to comparative advantage means that firms will have larger markets and will be enabled to grow larger, and hence have lower costs. This is a **dynamic process**, for large firms with low costs and high profits are able to invest in expensive research and development, *which enables these firms' productivity to continue to improve.* In fields of production involving complex modern technology only very large firms can afford to keep abreast of new developments and so compete successfully in world markets.

The most obvious gain from trade is the increased choice of goods for customers. If the UK had to be self-sufficient – unable for some reason to trade with other countries – the range of goods available would be greatly diminished. For example, it is possible to produce bananas

How to make comparative advantage work for you

These days politicians all over the world declare themselves in favour of *free trade*. When it comes to voting for it, they are not so sure. The reason is not just the pressure of special-interest politics. It is also that most people have imbibed the prejudice that free trade is a good thing, without imbibing the economics that ought to lie behind it. What this prejudice says, in fact, is that free trade is a good thing only if everybody else joins in; one-sided, or unilateral, free trade is a mug's game. The classical case for free trade argues exactly the opposite: *free trade is good for a country even if other countries do not return the favour.*

Writing 40 years before Ricardo, Adam Smith had already had a lot to say about the gains from trade. He saw it as, among other things, a way of promoting efficiency, both because it fostered competition and because it provided opportunities to specialise and gain economies of scale. Specialisation was a matter of absolute advantage: trade allows countries to produce what they are best at, and buy in the rest.

This view begged a question: what if Britain, say, is bad at making everything? Does this not mean that trade would drive all its producers out of business? David Ricardo answered the question by formulating the principle of comparative advantage. *This is perhaps the single most powerful idea in economics.*

Suppose there are two countries, Utopia and Flatland, and that these countries produce just two goods, wine and cheese. In Utopia it takes one hour of labour to make a pound of cheese and two hours to make a gallon of wine. In Flatland it takes six hours to make a pound of cheese and three hours to make a gallon of wine. Note that Utopia is more productive than Flatland in both goods; it has an absolute advantage in wine and cheese. But its greater advantage, its comparative advantage, is in cheese. This will determine what happens when the two countries trade.

The precise outcome will depend on the pattern of demand, and hence on the price of each good in terms of the other once trade begins. Assume that a pound of cheese trades for a gallon of wine. This is for simplicity's sake; the argument does not turn on the price chosen. In Utopia, which is better at making both goods, an hour of labour can make either a pound of cheese or a gallon of wine. But since a pound of cheese can be traded for a gallon of wine, it makes sense for Utopia to specialise in producing cheese, and then trade some of its cheese for wine. In this way it can consume as much cheese as before and twice as much wine, or some combination of more wine and cheese.

Flatland is less efficient than Utopia at making both goods. But in Flatland too it pays to specialise. An hour of its labour can make one-sixth of a pound of cheese or one-third of a gallon of wine (which is worth one-third of a pound of cheese in the international market). So Flatland specialises in the production of wine, and trades some of its wine for cheese. Trade means that it can consume as much wine as before and twice as much cheese, or some combination of more of both.

The example has been borrowed, by the way, from an excellent textbook, *International Economics,* written by Paul Krugman and Maurice Obstfeld. In parts of the real world, though, the free-trade debate still seems to be struggling. Krugman and Obstfeld quote with amusement an article from the *Wall Street Journal* ('The coming overthrow of free trade') which observed, 'Many small countries have no comparative advantage in anything.'

Source: *The Economist,* 2 September 1990

in a hothouse, but only at such high cost that few would be able to buy them. If your breakfast today included cornflakes, and tea or coffee, what would you have had instead of these imported products?

Completely free trade benefits all participants, so why then is trade restricted by **tariffs** and other measures? There are four basic reasons:

- ignorance
- selfishness
- health
- strategic arguments.

Ignorance of the real economic facts is possible because decisions are not taken by economists but by politicians – often on the basis of a wide variety of fallacious economic arguments.

More likely is *selfishness*: imagine that a major employer in your locality is suffering competition from imported goods and is consequently soon to become bankrupt. The local Member of Parliament persuades the government to intervene by assisting the uncompetitive firm. What assistance is likely? A subsidy would underline the firm's uncompetitive situation and so be inadvisable, but a tariff on imports would reduce or remove the imports (often described as 'unfair' competition) and raise prices, thus returning the firm to profitability and ensuring the jobs of its employees. But such a tariff is little different from a subsidy in that it enables an uncompetitive firm to survive. A major difference is that a subsidy is paid for by taxpayers making it obvious and unacceptable, whilst a tariff is paid for by consumers through higher prices (and reduced supplies) which seem to go unnoticed. Clearly a tariff benefits a minority at the expense of society in general. Those about to go bankrupt or lose their jobs are vociferous, whilst consumers are more dispersed and unorganised and so make no effective complaint. Consequently protective tariffs are exceedingly common.

The third reason for trade barriers is to protect *public health*. Such trade restrictions are intended to ensure that imported canned products, for example, meet reasonable health standards, and clearly *some* measures of this type are justified.

Finally, *strategic* reasons for protective tariffs or subsidies refer to a country's need to safeguard its food supply, and manufacturing industries capable of producing guns, aircraft and ships in case of war; this is clearly not an *economic* justification.

Effects of tariff removal in a customs union

Referring to Figure 2, P_1 is the initial price in say the UK, domestic supply is Q_{S1} and consumption Q_{D1}. As a result of the removal of an

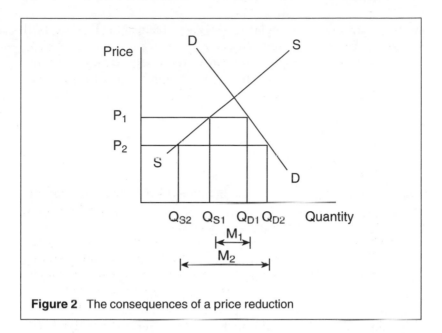

Figure 2 The consequences of a price reduction

import tariff after joining the customs union the price falls to P_2 and consumption rises to Q_{D2} whilst domestically produced supply falls to Q_{S2}. Clearly consumers are better off because they now consume more of the good at a lower price. The resources which had been devoted to producing Q_{S1}–Q_{S2} are released for the production of other goods. Imports have increased from M_1 to M_2, the extra coming from another member or other members of the customs union where there is a comparative advantage in the production of this good. Similarly, for some other good for which the UK has a comparative advantage, tariff removal in other member states will provide the UK with an expanded market and the production of this other good will employ the resources released by the contraction of production of the first good. **Trade creation** is the term given to such cases; clearly it benefits all members of the customs union.

Trade diversion is a potential disadvantage of joining a customs union. Remember that when the tariffs on trade between members are removed, they are replaced by common tariffs between the group and the rest of the world. So the common external tariff may mean that a country buys a particular good from its fellow members although it previously imported it more cheaply from a third country. It is intuitively obvious that, provided that the common external tariff adopted is not higher on average than the previous tariffs of member states which it replaces, the gains from trade creation will exceed the losses from trade diversion.

This analysis has been conducted in terms of tariffs. Clearly the gains from tariff removal are applicable to the removal of any other forms of trade barriers.

Economic integration

There are five levels of **economic integration** between countries. *Inevitably each implies a degree of political integration which could be regarded as some pooling of sovereignty.*

• Preference areas

These are agreements to give privileged access to certain products from specified countries. Thus, following the Ottawa Conference of 1932, a system of Imperial Preference was introduced for trade between the UK and countries of the British Empire. This involved a **reciprocal reduction** of tariffs on trade between the participants, although tariffs against outsiders remained relatively high. Imperial Preference was designed to help the exports of agricultural products from the Empire to Britain, and the exports of British manufacturers to the Empire. The **Lomé convention** has since 1975 given preferential access to the EU market for some products of certain developing countries. In this instance the preferential treatment is one-way, and is regarded as a form of development aid.

• Free trade areas

Here, trade in an agreed list of products occurs freely between the members of the free trade area, although members retain their independent tariffs against third countries. *Such an arrangement is an attempt to gain the benefits of comparative advantage and specialisation with a minimal loss of sovereignty.* The political content of an agreement is limited to rules which are necessary for its fair operation. The European Free Trade Area which the UK joined in 1960 is a good example (see Chapter 1).

• Customs union

This extends the free trade area idea to include a **common external tariff** against third countries. However, it involves far more political cooperation than does a free trade area. For example, the member states have to agree on the levels of tariff set and on their revision. This will obviously involve joint trade negotiations with third countries.

• Common market

This adds **freedom of movement for factors of production** (labour and capital) to the free trade in goods and services of a customs union. Proper application of the law of comparative advantage requires that there are no distortions to competition. Consequently much common policy formulation is required and so a great deal of political cooperation is essential.

• Economic and monetary union

A common market between member states having separate currencies still involves some internal trade barriers. These are **transactions costs** and **uncertainty**. The former relate to the cost of buying and selling currencies which are obviously part of any trade in goods and services. Uncertainty arises because exchange rates can alter between the time when a deal is planned and the time when it is executed, and such a change may turn profit into loss. The full exploitation of comparative advantage is only possible if there is a single currency. Thus economic and monetary union describes the situation when two or more countries unite their economies completely. *In turn this implies political*

The Single European Act

In December 1985, the European Council (the Heads of State or Government) meeting in Luxembourg, decided to give new impetus to European integration by drawing up a 'Single European Act', which was signed in February 1986 and came into force on 1 July 1987.

The Single Act is a new Treaty which modifies and supplements the Treaties of Paris and Rome (which established the three European Communities: ECSC, EEC, Euratom). Its aim is to bring the Community into line with the needs of the 1990s and to shape it into one large economic unit, a truly frontierless internal market with a population of 320 million: the biggest in the world.

Acting on the fact that Europe's lack of integration is proving expensive to the citizens of the Community (cost-ing between ECU 125 and 190 thousand million per year according to studies carried out by the Commission), the decision-makers in the Member States have decided to do everything possible to create, by 1 January 1993, a 'vast single market'. Citizens of the Twelve will be able to live and work in the country of their choice, regardless of what job they do. Tourists and travellers will be able to travel without frontier checks and use their credit cards in all the countries of the Community. Businesses will have a far wider market, leading to greater profitability from investment and the creation of employment – in short, an area in which there will be total freedom of movement for persons, goods and capital.

Source: *Europe in Figures*, 1989/90 edn, Eurostat

union also, for the effective control of an economy covers the money supply, taxation, the redistribution of incomes – in short, all the major economic decisions undertaken by a modern state.

• Expected economic benefits of the EU

As discussed in the previous chapter, the removal of tariff barriers is a necessary but not sufficient condition for free trade. The EU failed to follow up its initial removal of tariffs on internal trade with the required complementary measures, and so after an initial decade of rapid growth, relative stagnation set in. The **Single European Act** was passed in 1986 to remedy this situation. It aimed at the removal of *all* trade barriers by the end of 1992 in a programme which is discussed in the next chapter.

As the accompanying boxed article (on page 21) from *Europe in Figures* indicates, the Single European Market was estimated to make the EU substantially better off. EU GDP and employment were predicted to increase whilst inflation would be slightly reduced. These are '**static benefits**' – those that should be achieved within the first few years. In the long term the **dynamic benefit** was an expected increase of about one percentage point in the rate of economic growth. A 1996 Commission Report (COM(96) 520) estimates that the following benefits are directly attributable to the introduction of the Single Market:

- an extra 300,000 to 900,000 jobs
- an extra increase in GDP of 1.1–1.5% over the period 1987–93
- reduction in inflation rates of 1.0–1.5%.

Conclusion

This chapter has concentrated on the theoretical gains from comparative advantage. The gains *expected* turn out to be impressively large, and the Commission study noted above suggests that these gains *can be achieved in practice*, but *how* has the EU attempted to capture them, and are the gains *equitably distributed?* We now turn to these questions in the next few chapters.

KEY WORDS

Law of comparative advantage
Economies of size
Dynamic process
Tariffs
Trade creation
Trade diversion
Economic integration
Reciprocal reduction

Lomé convention
Common external tariff
Transaction costs
Uncertainty
Single European Act
Static benefits
Dynamic benefit

Further reading
Bamford, C. (ed.). Chapter 11 in *Economics for AS*. CUP, 2000.
Bamford, C. and Grant, S. Chapters 2 and 5 in *The UK Economy in a Global Context*. Heinemann Educational, 2000.
Smith, D. Chapter 9 in *UK Current Economic Policy* (2nd edn). Heinemann, Educational, 1999.

Useful website
EU's official website: www.europa.eu.int

Essay topics
1. (a) Referring to the European experience, explain how the formation of a customs union can create and divert trade.   [10 marks]
   (b) Comment upon the other likely economic effects of the formation of a customs union.   [10 marks]
   [UCLES, Economics of Europe Paper, Q3, June 1996.]
2. (a) Examine the factors which determine the value of a country's imports.   [50 marks]
   (b) Explain the policies which a country in the EU can pursue to reduce the value of its imports.   [50 marks]
   [Edexcel, Paper 2, Q6, January 1998.]

Data response question

The European Postal Services Industry

There has been debate in recent years about the possibility of opening up European postal services to competition. The extract below refers to the prospects for such liberalisation of the European postal services industry.

The greatest obstacle to a proper single market in the European Union is surely the existence of state-owned monopolies, like postal services.

European postal services share the obligation of 'universal service', the idea that it should cost the writer no more to send a letter to the most remote address in the land than to the house next door. Those who are sceptical of liberalisation fear that a postal free-for-all, on top of the competition they already face from faxes and e-mail, would make a universal service unaffordable. Hence their determination to keep their 'reserved areas' as legal monopolies.

Like many monopolies, though, Europe's state-owned postal services are often inefficient. Somehow more room must be found for more forms of competition from private sector courier services and other similar firms.

The Commission has proposed a two-stage reform: the immediate liberalisation of all mail that weighs more than 350 grams or is priced at more than five times the standard letter rate; and, from 2001, the liberalisation of 'direct' (junk) and cross-border mail.

Table 1 A comparison of Europe's postal services in 1994

	Number of postal staff	Domestic letter traffic (billion)	Costs ($ billion)	Revenues ($ billion)	Price index for letters up to 100 g (EU average = 100)
Germany	342 413	18.32	na	12.25	138
France	289 156	23.87	na	na	105
Italy*	221 534	6.62	5.63	4.13	130
Britain	189 000	16.75	5.83	6.29	84
Spain	65 355	4.06	0.92	0.87	32

*1993 figures.
na = data not available.

(a) (i) What is meant by a 'single market' in the context of the European Union? [2 marks]

(ii) With reference to the article, explain how state-owned postal services are obstacles to a 'proper single market'.

[3 marks]

(b) Why might the obligation to provide a 'universal service' be unattractive to private-sector firms? [2 marks]

(c) (i) Explain **one** reason why state-owned monopolies might be viewed as inefficient. [2 marks]

(ii) Use the data in Table 1 to compare the relative performance of Europe's postal services. [5 marks]

(d) Using economic analysis, discuss whether the possible effects of any liberalisation of European postal services would be beneficial. [6 marks]

Chapter Three

The Single Market

'Non tariff barriers are effective trade barriers. Before the Single European Act it would have taken an accountant 50 years to qualify and requalify in each member country so as to be able to audit in each country!'

This chapter examines how free competition within the EU – the Single Market – can be achieved; it involves removing many other impediments as well as tariffs on internal trade before goods and services can flow freely. The Single Market also has significant social implications, which are also noted.

Internal competition
It should be remembered that a common market involves the free movement of goods, services, capital and labour between a group of countries. Emphasis is to be laid on the word *free*, both here and in the term free competition. *Only in a free market can comparative advantage, specialization and concomitant economies of size be attained.*

Economies of size in many fields of industrial production can be gained only by very large firms, much larger than those existing within the EU when it was formed. This implies either the growth of some firms, and the demise of their internal competitors, or their growth by merger and acquisition regardless of member state boundaries. Unfortunately the arrival of 'European firms' large enough to compete successfully in world markets with the largest American and Japanese firms requires the removal of national legal, technical and fiscal barriers by **harmonization** (an important EU concept which has sometimes threatened curious anomalies), *implying the replacement of national by Union-wide laws, standards and taxes.*

Harmonization in the industrial field has turned out to be extremely slow and difficult – this was one of the factors behind the introduction of the Single European Act (SEA) already mentioned, and discussed in detail below. The only significant industrial activity undertaken at Community level before the SEA was its assistance to declining industries, steel being the major example. The European steel industry suffered from chronic excess capacity and lack of international competitiveness. Its reduction in size and its modernization were coordinated by the EU, greatly assisted by the existence of the

European Coal and Steel Community, which provided the necessary mechanisms.

Removing tariffs on internal trade is a necessary but not sufficient condition for free internal trade. A plethora of non-tariff barriers (NTBs) and state aids can effectively prevent or greatly reduce trade. NTBs include different technical standards and complex documentation. Before the single market, the manufacturer of a product might have to produce it in twelve different versions to satisfy the different national criteria of the then twelve members states, and similarly provide different documentation for each member state, involving several languages. There are many other ways in which internal trade may be distorted, and the one which attracts most attention is state aid. Helping industries through the provision of production subsidies, artificially low interest rates, research and development expenditures and so on, may be legitimate (though economically dubious) government activities, but if practised differently by the individual member states competition will obviously be distorted.

Competition policy

The discussion so far has focused on national government policies, but private firms can also indulge in practices which distort competition. Price fixing and market sharing cartels are the prime examples. Indeed, the initiation of the 1992 Programme encouraged such a rash of mergers and acquisitions across national frontiers that some analysts asked if these were to capture the benefits of large scale production or represented the cartelisation of Europe.

National governments have long had their own measures to combat cartels. The Community leaves the control of cartels within member states to the members themselves unless there is an appreciable effect on trade between members. In the latter case *the Commission has wide powers to prohibit agreements intended to prevent, restrict or distort competition within the Single Market*.

Similarly, the Commission can prevent a firm which has a '**dominant position**' (e.g. a monopoly) from abusing that position. Note that having a dominant position *is* permitted – indeed the Community wishes to see more very large European firms capable of competing with the largest foreign firms in the world market; it is only the *abuse* of dominance which is prohibited.

Control over mergers and acquisitions which might give rise to a dominant position was agreed in 1989 along the following lines. Any firms whose desired merger seems likely to meet the regulation's criteria must notify the Commission of their proposals. The Commission

A textbook cartel that broke all the rules

For months, Europe's unsubsidised steel makers have denounced the underhand way some governments finance their weaker brethren. Now they themselves have been found guilty of dirty tricks. On February 16th, in what he dubbed 'a textbook cartel case that broke every rule,' Karel Van Miert, the European Union's competition commissioner, announced record fines totalling 104m ecus ($117m) against 16 companies for rigging the market in steel beams.

The ringleaders in the cartel included British Steel (which was fined 32m ecus), and Unimetal, part of France's Usinor Sacilor group (12.3m ecus). According to Mr Van Miert, the steel makers used their cosy Brussels club, Eurofer, to put the cartel together virtually under the noses of his trust-busters. The steelmen also spun a web of bilateral deals among themselves, agreeing upon prices, staying out of each other's markets and exchanging confidential commercial information. The commission can fine firms up to 10% of their turnover in the market affected. The figure for British Steel was the equivalent of 7%, one of the highest rates ever imposed.

Source: *The Economist*, 19 February 1994

will decide within one month whether to start proceedings and will then have four months in which to reach a final decision. Satisfying three criteria will cause the Commission to act:

- merging firms have a combined world turnover exceeding 5 bn Ecu (£3.6bn)
- at least 250m Ecu of turnover is generated within the EU
- less than two thirds of the combined turnover comes from one member state.

The last criterion means that mergers with no major EU dimension remain the responsibility of national authorities such as the UK's Monopolies and Mergers Commission.

The EU Commission vet proposed mergers against the concept of a dominant position which significantly impedes effective competition. The regulation deals with any form of concentration of economic power and thus may include partial mergers and some joint ventures.

This regulation was reviewed in 1994. It remained unchanged despite the Commission's wish to extend its powers to mergers over 3 bn Ecu. The boxed article from *The Economist* of 19 February 1994 gives an example of the policy in action.

The Single European Act and 1992 Programme

In Chapter 1, the SEA was described as the 'relaunching' of the Community. It was necessitated by the effect of non-tariff barriers (NTBs) preventing the free movement of goods, services, capital and labour within the Community, and the slow progress made towards the removal of these barriers under the unanimity system of decision making. In 1985 the European Council agreed to this Act to remove NTBs and create a single European market by the end of 1992.

The SEA amended the Treaty of Rome, and came into force on 1 July 1987. Since then NTBs have been progressively removed over a wide field, decisions being greatly speeded by the adoption of a system of majority voting (see Chapter 1).

Purchasing by governments and other public bodies accounts for about 15 per cent of EU GDP. Traditionally such purchases have been almost exclusively from national suppliers and contractors. As part of the 1992 programme such **public procurement** has been the subject of new directives which aim to ensure that all companies in the EU have a fair chance of tendering for such contracts regardless of national frontiers. These directives prohibit discriminatory specifications and complex tendering procedures, force major contracts to be advertised at EU level with reasonable time limits for bids to be received. Purchasers must be prepared to justify their rejection of bids, and complaints can be taken to the Court. Electricity generating equipment and railway equipment are typical of the sectors most affected by these rules. Traditionally each national public authority favoured its national champions, with the consequence that intra-EU trade in such products was very small, price differences between member states were substantial and rates of capacity utilization were low. Clearly, because of the huge potential economies of size in these sectors, the single market rules were expected to lead to a major restructuring through mergers, concentration, and closure of plants. Indeed the Single Market lead to an immediate explosion of mergers and acquisitions both within and and between states. Increasing concentration often enables firms to raise prices, but the increase in competition which the Single Market engendered has tended to reduce prices.

In the long term the EU aims to harmonize business laws and technical standards but this is a very slow process. In the short term some pragmatic changes have been introduced to free markets from legal and technical NTBs. Thus, a standard **Single European Document** has been introduced to accompany goods being sent across national frontiers, replacing a plethora of complex different national documents. Most important on the technical front is the principle that what is acceptable in one member state must be acceptable in others. For example, in Germany, regulations insist that beer must be made from water, malt and hops only; all other additives are prohibited, and so Germany refused to permit beer imports from other member states. The Court of Justice ruled that not withstanding their national rules, the Germans must permit the import of beers from other members – additives and all – provided that such beers met with the national standards in their countries of origin. This principle of **mutual recognition** is the key which has unlocked the door to the free movement of goods long before European standards can be agreed.

Financial services is one of the most rapidly growing sectors of the European economies but cross frontier competition was prevented by NTBs. Consequently this sector was targeted in the 1992 Programme. Its liberalisation was expected to contribute one third of all the economic gains from the introduction of the single market. Two factors explain the lack of competition in financial services. First, cross frontier competition was impossible so long as national governments maintained capital exchange controls. Second, each government had its own regulatory framework. Regulation in this sector is essential, to control the money supply for example, and to protect bank depositors from fraud.

The Treaty of Rome called for the free movement of goods, labour and *capital*, but for more than thirty years little was done to promote

Table 3 EU member states' trade with other members as a percentage of their total trade in 1958 and 1998

	Imports		Exports	
	1958	*1998*	*1958*	*1998*
Belgium/Luxembourg	56	71	55	76
Denmark	60	70	59	67
Germany*	36	58	38	56
Greece	54	65	51	51
Spain	32	69	47	71
France	28	68	31	62
Ireland	69	62	82	70
Italy	30	62	35	56
Netherlands	51	58	58	79
Austria	-	73	-	63
Portugal	53	77	39	82
Finland	-	66	-	56
Sweden	-	69	-	58
United Kingdom	22	53	22	58
Total EU15	-	63	-	63

* 1958 West Germany, 1998 unified Germany.

Source: *European Economy 63*, 1997; *Eurostat Yearbook*, 2000.

freedom for capital because of the autonomy of national monetary authorities and potential or actual balance of payments problems. However, in 1993 all controls on exchange and capital movements were removed. A directive was introduced to liberalise trade in areas such as stocks and shares, unit trusts, money market instruments and financial futures. In 1994 a new EU banking licence system made it much easier for banks based in one state to open branches in other parts of the Community. However, capital taxes are part of national direct taxation which is not subject to harmonisation. So different rates of capital taxation could distort competition if the differences were large.

The gradual liberalisation of intra-EU trade has brought about very large increases in trade between members countries. Table 3 provides the data to support this claim.

Tax harmonisation

Tax policy is part of a country's overall economic policy, financing public spending and redistributing income. In the EU, tax policy remains the responsibility of its members; some taxing power is often delegated to regional or local levels. The EU's role is not to standardise national taxes and social security contributions but only to ensure that they do not distort competition in any way, or interfere with the free movement of goods, services, and capital. Table 4 shows that there is considerable diversity in the structure and rates of compulsory taxes and social contributions between member states, with a difference of just over 20 percentage points between the highest level of taxes (54.1% in Sweden) and the lowest (33.9% in Greece). Indirect taxes are VAT and excise duties, direct tax is mainly income tax, and social contributions are 'taxes on employment', which are paid partly by employees and partly by employers. Social contributions may have a direct impact on employment, so the structure of taxation is important as well as the total level.

Article 99 of the Treaty of Rome called for the harmonisation of indirect taxation, but the only major progress in this direction has been the adoption of VAT (based on the previous French system) as the *method* of collection. The harmonization of *rates* of tax and excise duty is proving to be a particularly intractable problem, although members have committed themselves to this in principle as one of the provisions of the Single European Act. Progress is hindered by the fact that all fiscal decisions are still subject to unanimity in the Council of Ministers. Differences in VAT rates are considerable and through their effect on market prices clearly distort competition. Rates of excise duties (on alcohol, tobacco and fuel) vary even more. Table 5 gives

31

Table 4 Taxes and social security contributions as % of GDP in 1997

	Indirect taxes	Direct taxes	Social contributions	Total
Belgium	12.8	18.8	15.5	46.6
Luxembourg	17.2	16.6	11.8	45.6
Denmark	19.2	32.2	1.7	53.1
Germany	12.6	10.1	18.9	41.6
Greece	15.1	9.0	9.8	33.9
Spain	11.1	12.1	13.0	36.2
France	15.8	11.3	19.2	46.3
Ireland	14.8	14.7	4.6	34.1
Italy	12.8	16.6	15.1	44.5
Netherlands	13.6	13.4	18.9	45.9
Austria	16.0	13.6	15.3	44.9
Portugal	15.3	10.6	12.0	37.9
Finland	15.8	11.3	19.2	46.3
Sweden	16.2	22.8	15.1	54.1
United Kingdom	14.2	15.0	6.7	35.9
Total EU15	13.8	13.7	15.1	42.6

Source: *Tax policy in the European Union*, European Communities, 2000.

VAT rates and excise duties on still wine, demonstrating some major differences in tax regimes. For cigarettes the complicated structure of VAT and duties make it easier to appreciate country differences by looking at the normal retail selling prices, and these are given in the table. Fuel prices vary less, but because of the significance of transport costs in the cost of many goods, differences are more price-distorting. Taking unleaded petrol as indicative of fuel tax differentials, the highest taxes (hence prices) in November 2000 were in the UK with an excise duty of 783.04 Euros per 1000 litres and VAT at 17.5%. Greece had the lowest taxes, with an excise duty of 307.32 Euros and VAT at 18%.

For many years, different VAT and excise duty rates resulted in member states maintaining border formalities to collect taxes on imports and refund them on exports on intra-EU trade. Clearly this made nonsense of the single market for many goods. In 1994 border formalities were replaced by other bureaucratic procedures to speed trade movements but it still left the distortions.

The boxed extract from the *Nottingham Evening Post* (p. 34) takes a humorous look at the consequences of huge differences in member

Table 5 Rates of VAT and excise duty on still wine and unleaded petrol, November 2000

| | Still wine | | Cigarettes |
	VAT %	Excise duties (Euro)	Current most popular price category per 1000 (Euro)
Belgium	21	47.10	140.8
Luxembourg	12	0.00	104.12
Denmark	25	94.84	201.79
Germany	16	0.00	134.55
Greece	18	0.00	98.89
Spain	16	0.00	84.14
France	19.6	3.35	147.88
Ireland	21	273.01	234.27
Italy	20	0.00	95.54
Netherlands	17.5	48.78	121.61
Austria	20	0.00	119.91
Portugal	5	0.00	87.29
Finland	22	235.46	189.21
United Kingdom	17.5	237.53	324.67

Source: *Excise tables*, European Communities, 2000.

states' alcohol excise duties in 1993. In 2000 these distortions still remain. Indeed UK Customs and Excise claim that cigarette smuggling is now cheating the Exchequer of £2.5 billion per year (and as many smuggled cigarettes are very carinogenic high tar brands or counterfeits there are other costs to both the consumers and health services).

Social aspects of competition

Initially social policy concentrated on retraining workers who became unemployed in the 1960s as a result of structural changes during this early period of rapid economic growth. More recently the **European Social Fund** has become one of the structural funds which are intended to help to redistribute more equitably the gains from freer competition; this aspect of social policy is discussed as part of regional policy in Chapter 5. In the current chapter we are concerned with distortions of competition which may arise as a result of differing national social conditions, and rights of workers.

The Commission felt that the introduction of the single market, with its stimulation of business, should be balanced by the develop-

Get loaded on 'Booze Cruise'

C'est formidable. The French have finally revealed how much beer they sold the British this year – nearly 16 pints for every person of drinking age.

A year after cross-Channel trade barriers came down and the British began going to France en masse for cheap drink, the figures prove conclusively that Brits like their beer as much as the French like their wine. Especially at those prices.

Victory

The trend also poses a growing threat to the traditional British pub and off-licence, both of which are starting to feel the pinch now that one pint in every eight drunk at home is imported – legally or illegally – from France.

It is hard to say who can claim victory in the latterday Norman Conquest that has seen 120,000 Britons crossing the Channel each week from Dover to Calais.

It is certainly a mutually beneficial arrangement. The French hypermarkets rake in the cash from British beer buyers and the ferry companies are making a packet from the booming cross-Channel 'Booze Cruise', which transports 18 tons of beer back to Britain every day.

The drinkers have been saving a fortune in duty, while profiteers can cash in further by selling beer illegally at a profit back home – thanks to the law that allows unlimited amounts of beer to be brought over for 'personal use'.

How can Customs prove you are not buying a year's supply? The only definite losers are the Government, who charge 30p per pint in duty, compared with 4p in France.

The UK – Europe's second-cheapest producer of beer after Portugal – now charges the second highest rate of duty after Ireland, with one-third of the cost of every pint going to the Exchequer in duty and VAT.

So much beer is being brought in from France that no one can produce accurate figures. But wildly differing figures from each side of the Channel are both far higher than all pre-Christmas estimates.

The chamber of commerce in Calais estimates that 500 million litres of beer, wine and spirits have been sold so far this year, of which up to 80 per cent is beer. In English pub measures, that's 712 million pints.

The Brewers' Society estimates that a more conservative 150 million litres of beer – a mere 263 million pints – will have come in from France alone during 1993.

Output

But that is still more than the annual output of a British brewery like Youngs and Fullers, and the loss in excise duty to the Government will be around £240 million. With wine and spirits, the figure doubles to almost £500 million.

Brewers' Society spokesman Mike Ripley said: 'The problem is that we just pay too much tax on booze here.

'We are not just out of line with the rest of Europe, we are way out of line. And as long as there is that incentive, you will have people going abroad to buy it more cheaply'.

Source: *Nottingham Evening Post,* 1 January 1994

ment of social conditions which would ensure that all citizens would benefit. The economic programme was to be given a 'human face'. Accordingly, the Social Charter was produced, its first draft appearing in May 1989. It was discussed in June by the Economic and Social Affairs Committee followed by the European Council. It was broadly welcomed by eleven member states but opposed by the UK. The Council made the following three points:

- In the construction of the single market, social aspects should be accorded the same importance as economic aspects.
- In the creation of the single market, job creation should be given top priority.
- Implementation should comply with the principle of 'subsidiarity'.

The UK seized upon the term 'subsidiarity' and took it to heart, claiming that the whole topic was best dealt with by member states. The principle of subsidiarity, which the Social Charter introduced, was also included in Article 3B of the Treaty of Maastricht. It means that action should only be taken at the European level if a given objective could not better be achieved by member states. In theory the principle applies to all levels, thus national government should allow local government to take decisions whenever possible. Whilst the UK's Conservative government seized eagerly upon the principle in so far as it affected its dealings with the EU, it usually ignored it completely in its dealings with local government within the UK. However the Labour government elected in 1997 has been more sympathetic to the principle, actually delegating some powers to new regional government assemblies in Scotland and Wales.

The Social Charter listed the 'fundamental rights' of EU workers, most of which already existed in the other member states, but several of which did not exist in the UK. For example, there was no statutory right to annual paid leave in the UK, although this right already existed in all other members except Italy. Similarly, only the UK and Denmark did not impose a limit on working hours (as publicity given to the hours worked by junior hospital doctors may remind us). There was no statutory right to strike in the UK, and works councils were not compulsory.

The social concerns of the other member states produced a follow up to the Charter. They attempted to get its main provisions included in the Maastricht Treaty. Once again the UK refused and the outcome was a protocol to the Treaty permitting the UK to ignore the Social Charter.

Why was the UK government so opposed to these social aspects of the EU? It claimed that implementation of the implied social policies would raise costs of production and make Europe uncompetitive. In support of these claims it noted that foreign countries' investment in Europe was being concentrated in the UK because of its refusal to adopt the EU's social aspirations. This is tantamount to admitting that the UK's attitude caused distortion to fair competition! But times and attitudes change – one of the first actions of the Labour government elected in 1997 was to announce its intention to sign up to the EU's social policy. Accordingly, in 1997, under the Amsterdam Treaty, the Community Treaties were amended to include the social protocol. The significance of social security provisions is considered in Chapter 7 in the context of globalisation.

Consequences of the Single Market

Reaping the advantages of economies of size, and of increased competition, brought about by the liberalisation of intra-European trade, was expected to bring handsome economic returns. An *ex ante* Commission report (the Cecchini Report 'The Economics of 1992'), estimated the benefits to be expected from the Single Market programme as increases in GDP of 4.5% to 6%, price reductions of 6% and the creation of an extra 1,750,000 jobs, plus an improvement in the external balance. Have these expectations been fulfilled? Certainly liberalisation brought about dramatic increases in the pace of mergers and acquisitions as firms sought to benefit from size economies. However, both the Cecchini *ex ante* estimates and later *ex post* studies are subject to wide margins of error, and it is difficult to say how much of the changes which have occurred are due to the single market and which would have happened anyway. Despite problems of estimation, the concensus is that the single market has had a substantial positive affect.

Conclusion

Liberalisation of intra-European trade has lead to considerable increases in trade flows. The single market key has been the principle of mutual recognition. Mutual recognition applies to individuals, food, goods and services, for example, an accountant or any other professional who is qualified in one member state can work in any of the others. The lack of fiscal harmonisation remains as a major competition-distorting problem.

KEY WORDS

Harmonization   Single European Document
Dominant position   Mutual recognition
Public procurement   European Social Fund

Further reading
Bamford, C. (ed.). Chapter 12 in *Economics for AS*. CUP, 2000.
Grant, S. Chapter 64 in *Stanlake's Introductory Economics*, (7th edn).
Longman, 2000.
Sloman, J. Chapter 23 in *Economics*, (4th edn). Pearson Education.

Useful website
EU's official journal: www.europa.eu.int/eur-lex

Essay topics
1. (a) Explain the term 'economic integration'.   [8 marks]
   (b) Discuss how economists might analyse the effects of economic integration upon the economics of Europe.   [12 marks]
   [UCLES, Economics of Europe paper, Q3, June 1997.]
2. Common policies are an important part of economic integration as practised in the European Union (EU).
   (a) Explain, using examples, why the EU has adopted common policies.   [10 marks]
   (b) With reference to a single example of your choice, discuss the extent to which a common policy has been successful in its aims.   [10 marks]
   [OCR, Economics of Europe paper, Q3, March 2000.]

Data response question

Section B

Answer **one** question from this section.

Examine Figures 1–6 which relate to the UK labour market.

Figure 1 Percentage of UK employees affected by the National Minimum Wage, by industry

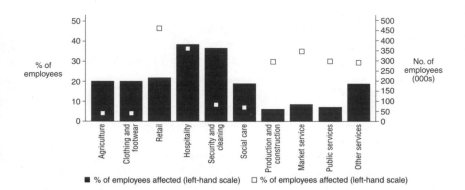

■ % of employees affected (left-hand scale) □ % of employees affected (left-hand scale)

Figure 2 Characteristics of the lowest paid, UK, 1997

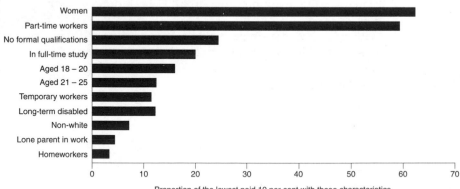

Proportion of the lowest paid 10 per cent with these characteristics
(Source: Report of the Low Pay Commission, June 1998.)

Figure 3 Percentage of employees who were temporary: UK, spring 1984 to spring 1996; not seasonally adjusted

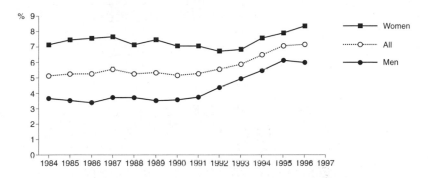

(Source: *Labour Market Trends*, September 1997.)

Figure 4 Percentage of population aged 65 and over

Figure 5 Average annual hours worked per person in employment

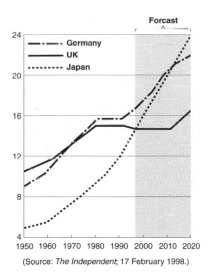

(Source: *The Independent*, 17 February 1998.)

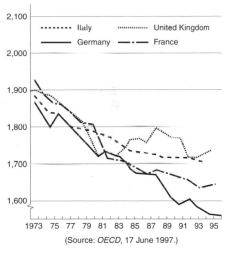

(Source: *OECD*, 17 June 1997.)

Figure 6 Hours worked by full-time employees and self-employed, UK, weekly, winter 1997–98

	Men	Women	All
People without a second job (000s)	13,092	6,330	19,422
Average weekly hours worked	39.0	33.7	37.2
People with a second job (000s)	414	240	654
Average weekly hours worked in both jobs	48.8	42.2	46.4

Notes: (i) Data based on respondents' own estimates, not actual hours worked.

     (ii) Data include paid and unpaid overtime but exclude meal breaks.

(Source: *Labour Market Trends*, August 1998.)

(a) How might the incidence of low pay in different industries shown in Figure 1 be explained, using the information in Figure 2?   [8 marks]

(b) With reference to Figure 3, identify the factors which might explain the trend in:

    (i)   the use of temporary workers by employers;

    (ii) the willingness of employees to accept temporary work.

[6 marks]

(c) Examine the economic implications of the trends shown in Figure 4 for both employers and the governments in these countries.   [7 marks]

(d) With reference to Figures 5 and 6, outline the likely economic effects on individual employees and employers of the UK complying with the EU directive of a maximum 48 hour working week.   [4 marks]

[Edexcel, Paper 3A, Q2, June 1999.]

Chapter Four

The Common Agricultural Policy

A market-rigging monument to economic folly

This chapter examines the policy developed in the original EEC of the six countries and its subsequent modifications. When the EEC began in 1958 about 20 per cent of its population was employed in agriculture, making this by far the largest industry. Each member state had its own agricultural policy. Harmonizing these policies was essential, otherwise they would result in different food prices in different countries, and this would distort competition – because wages are influenced by food prices. The need to develop a common agricultural policy is stated in Article 3 of the Treaty of Rome. It is the first common policy mentioned, underlining the importance attached to it. The need to unify existing disparate national policies is obvious, but why were agricultural policies needed anyway?

Reasons for agricultural policies

Returning to medieval times, most of the population was occupied by agriculture. The process of economic development involves the transfer of much of this labour force to other activities. Necessarily, the first requirement is for an increase in labour productivity in agriculture, so that some labour can be released. In practice land productivity increased along with that of labour, as food production increased; growing output meant declining food prices. Consequently the returns to agricultural resources in general declined. So resources were reallocated from agriculture to more profitable uses. History demonstrates that labour is persuaded to leave agriculture only slowly, resulting in incomes that are persistently below those of other occupations. In the twentieth century, low incomes for such a large sector of the economy came to be considered as inequitable, and so became the focus for government intervention. The low incomes are caused by economic forces, but policies to raise them are *social* not economic, although there are significant economic consequences.

An economic reason for intervention is that agricultural prices are inherently unstable in a free market. **Price elasticities** of demand for food products are low – because consumption of food means physical consumption, and once people are full a reduction in prices will not persuade them to eat much more. Neither will a rise in price greatly reduce their desire to eat. Imagine that the price elasticity of demand for potatoes is -0.1, in a particular year the yield of potatoes is low owing to drought and marketed output is reduced by 5 per cent. Clearly potato prices will rise and farmers can do nothing about it; extra potatoes can only be produced next year (i.e. the supply is perfectly inelastic in the short run). How much will prices rise? – with these data, 50 per cent! Thus, if the price elasticity of demand is low, which it is for most agricultural products, small changes in outputs cause relatively large changes in prices. Such unstable prices fail to tell producers what consumers really want. Some action to stabilize prices is therefore likely to result in an improvement in **economic efficiency**.

There is also a *strategic argument* for intervention. A secure food supply is an essential element of policy for any government and is neglected at a country's peril. The UK discovered this in the early years of last century. Comparative advantage had been followed resulting in the UK exporting manufactures and importing food – a sound economic policy which seemed safe as there had been peace in Europe for a hundred years. When the First World War began three-quarters of the flour in British bread was imported!

The Common Agricultural Policy

The aims of the policy as stated in Article 39 may be summarized as follows:

- to increase productivity
- to raise farm incomes
- to stabilize markets
- to assure the availability of supplies
- to ensure reasonable prices for consumers.

Although the Treaty of Rome does not make it clear, the fundamental objective is the raising of farm incomes and we now turn to the methods of achieving this – raising product prices and encouraging structural change.

Price support

The EEC decided that farmers' incomes were too low because their product prices were too low, and so it designed a policy to raise prices. Figure 3 relates to the situation in the 1960s when the policy was introduced. The supply and demand curves relate to EEC farmers and consumers. Free trade would result in a European price level of WP, standing for World Price. At this price Q_{S1} and Q_{D1} would be produced and consumed respectively, the difference being imported. The

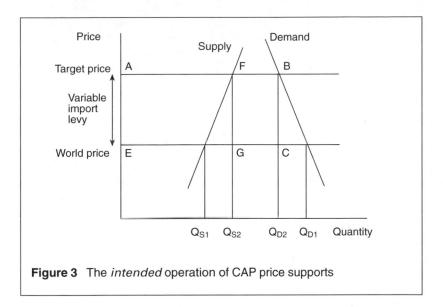

Figure 3 The *intended* operation of CAP price supports

EEC decided to raise the wholesale price to TP (**target price**). At this price farmers expand production to Q_{S2} and consumption declines to Q_{D2}. Cheap imports are prevented from undermining the target price by a **variable import levy** (VIL) which raises WP to at least TP.

The effects of the policy are to raise prices substantially – TP is much higher than WP – for the benefit of farmers. Prices are also stabilized, for if WP varies, the variable import levy is altered to compensate, thus keeping TP virtually constant. Consumers are worse off since they have to pay higher prices for less consumption; indeed the area ABCE (price difference times consumption) is an **implicit food tax**. Area FBCG (variable import levy times quantity imported) represents the revenue collected on imports which reduces the need for other taxation. The policy evidently transfers income from food consumers to farmers and taxpayers. Of course countries supplying imports are worse off as their market is diminished.

This support policy ignored time and the changes which it brings. Although the internal demand for food changed very little since the population remained almost constant, supplies continually expanded under the spur of technological progress, encouraged by the artificially high level of prices.

So in Figure 4 the supply curve has moved to the right, and at the administered price TP, production exceeds consumption even in the absence of imports. Originally the policy raised prices by reducing

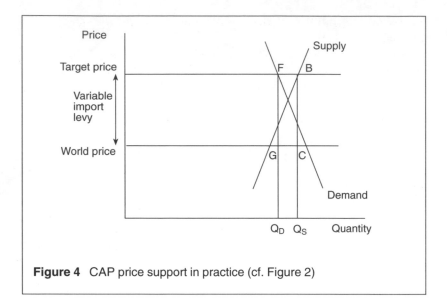

Figure 4 CAP price support in practice (cf. Figure 2)

imports; when imports have been reduced to zero as in this figure, what is to stop price falling below TP to the level indicated by the intersection of demand and supply? – an **intervention system.**

It was realized from the beginning that for many products a post-harvest glut would force market prices below TP even without imports. An intervention agency in each member state was formed to buy and store produce at intervention prices – set a little below target prices. Later in the season there would be seasonal shortages permitting the sale of the post-harvest surpluses.

But the situation in Figure 4 became the rule: supplies increased so much that surpluses were 'normal' instead of seasonal and they were purchased and stored with little likelihood of future release on to the internal market. These surpluses became known popularly as butter, beef and cereals mountains and wine lakes. Other products were also in surplus: there have been vegetable oil lakes and dried currant mountains for example. Comparing Figures 3 and 4, the major change is from net imports to surpluses. What became of the latter?

Most surpluses were exported. To make this possible **export subsidies** were provided equal to TP minus WP enabling traders to sell in world markets at world prices. Clearly this still involved a transfer of income from consumers to farmers, but now taxpayers had to pay for the removal of surpluses. Such '**dumping**' (i.e. selling abroad below cost) of EC surpluses disadvantaged third countries supplying food to the world market. On the other hand many food importers got marvellous bargains.

It should be noted that this price policy did nothing to make farming competitive in world terms. Indeed it accepted that European farming was uncompetitive and protected farmers from competition, which ensured that they never would become competitive. The difference in price levels between the internal and world markets became so large that fraud became widespread, and reputably the source of much income for the Mafia and the IRA!

Structural policy

Why was and is European agriculture uncompetitive? History bequeathed to Europe a very large number of farms, most being far too small to provide a reasonable income: small farms have high unit costs and produce little revenue. A farm can only expand to become a profitable business by increasing its land area, and as the supply of land is fixed it follows that an efficient agricultural industry means far fewer farms and *farmers*.

Here is the problem: there were, and are, millions of farmers, most of whom would need to leave the land before agriculture could become efficient. But agricultural labour mobility is notoriously low, and as farmers die or retire too many are replaced by a new generation.

Since the 1960s, to increase mobility, there have been measures for retraining farmers for other occupations or to help them to retire. But few wish to leave agriculture and too little money has been provided for this **structural policy** to have much impact. Enthusiasm for such policies was notably lacking in the early days of the EEC when the economies of the Six were expanding rapidly. The widespread unemployment of more recent years has made any restructuring of farming far more difficult. Quite simply, there have been no jobs for ex-farmers to go to; they might as well farm inefficiently as become unemployed.

Green currencies

The price support policy was completed in 1968 – that is, agricultural prices in the member states had been gradually changed until they reached common levels. But then, events conspired to upset these common prices.

A world system of fixed exchange rates had operated successfully for about 24 years, now it began to break up. The common prices for agricultural products were denominated in units of account (**European Currency Units**) which translated into member states' currencies at fixed rates. In 1969 the French franc was devalued and the German mark revalued. At the new currency values, since agricultural prices were in units of account the prices of French agricultural products should have increased (there are now more francs per unit of account) whilst German prices should have fallen.

Neither country was willing to permit these price changes, the French saying that higher food prices were inflationary and the Germans that lower prices would reduce farmers' incomes unacceptably. So although all other industries had to put up with the consequences of the currency changes the out-of-date currency values were retained in both countries just for agriculture; i.e. prices in France were lower and in Germany higher than the agreed common prices.

To prevent these price differences distorting trade in agricultural products, a system of border taxes and subsidies was introduced. These **monetary compensatory amounts** (MCAs) became increasingly important as currency changes became more frequent. As they permitted the use of artificial exchange rates for internal agricultural trade, these rates became known as **green currencies**.

It is ironic that in a common market, the size of the MCAs became so large that real price differences for agricultural products often exceeded those existing between member states before the EEC began. *This was clearly a serious distortion of competition – such price differences prevent the operation of comparative advantage.* MCAs were supposed to be abolished with the introduction of the single market at the end of 1992, but they weren't. They remained to distort the single market, and their ultimate removal was made more difficult as currency instability became prevalent during the 1990s.

Consequences of the CAP

Have its policy objectives been achieved? Certainly productivity has increased, and supplies have been assured, both partly the result of high prices. The manipulated price system has also stabilized prices. What is 'reasonable' cannot be objectively defined, so it is a matter of opinion whether or not prices to consumers have been reasonable.

What is beyond doubt is that *the primary objective of raising farm incomes to levels comparable to those of other sectors has not been achieved*. Before the inception of the CAP, and today, farmers on average have incomes about half of those of the non-farming members of society; the policy has completely failed to improve their relative position.

Averages always hide much information. In the present case consider who benefits most from higher prices – clearly the farmers who produce most. These large farmers also have lower unit production costs (economies of size). So the CAP has been helping the larger, relatively wealthy farmers, whilst leaving the poorer small farmers still poor. Also, the policy has transferred income from consumers to producers, including transfers from poor consumers – for even the poor must eat – to richer farmers! On equity grounds such income transfers have few supporters.

There are two other major areas affected by the CAP which must be considered: the financial and economic consequences. The financial consequences arise from the need to dispose of the surpluses generated by the high price system. These financial costs are met by the **Agricultural Guarantee and Guidance Fund** (AGGF) which has dominated the budget, as shown in Table 6. The huge expenditures on agricultural support mean that little has been left to finance other common policies. Consequently, the development of other policy areas has been hindered. However, the gradual introduction of reforms, discussed below, has stabilised agricultural support costs and reduced their share of the budget.

Table 6 Budgetary expenditure of the EU, selected years 1971–99 (million Ecus)

	Agricultural fund	Structural funds	Admini- stration	Other	Totals	Agriculture percentage share
1971	1884	57	132	152	2289	82
1979	10736	1268	864	1448	14603	74
1987	23939	5104	1740	3721	35469	67
1995	40247	19046	3691	7695	71955	56
1996	41328	26006	4128	10426	81888	50
1997	41305	26633	4284	10144	82366	50
1998	40937	28595	4353	9644	83529	49
1999	40940	30659	4502	9457	85558	48

Source: *European Economy*, vol. 69, 1999.

Economic efficiency

The economic consequences of the CAP are of two types – conventional and environmental. In terms of conventional economics, the fact that agriculture is much more heavily protected/subsidized than other industries means that it uses some resources which could be used more profitably elsewhere. Thus on the grounds of efficiency there is significant **resource misallocation** within the EU. As the other industrialized countries outside the EU have their own agricultural support systems, some even more protective than the CAP, the misallocation is of global significance. The protection of agriculture is believed to contribute to unemployment in EU manufacturing. It is argued that because the CAP expands EU agricultural production to the point of major dumping on world markets (EU is the world's second largest exporter of agricultural products) it must make countries which have a comparative advantage in agricultural production poorer. As a result their imports of manufactures from the EU are reduced, and it follows that so is employment in manufacturing industry. This problem is compounded by high food prices in the EU which help to raise costs via wages in other industries and damage their international competitiveness.

Green economics

Some of the environmental side-effects of the CAP merit a mention in passing. The CAP has encouraged, through its high prices, the ploughing of chalk downs in the south of England, and moors in parts of the north, which at world prices would have remained as grazing lands. Wild flowers, butterflies and many other insects, bird and mammal populations have been much reduced. Putting a monetary value on environmental amenities is notoriously difficult – how would you value a beautiful view, or a colony of rare wild flowers? Public attention tends to concentrate on the damage caused by the CAP, but it has its positive side too. Without the CAP's subsidization of livestock production in the remote and unprofitable regions of the EU – which account for huge areas of mountains, hills and moors etc. – agriculture would have disappeared from these regions. The loss of grazing animals would have resulted in the replacement of pleasant alpine meadows, for example, by unsightly bracken and scrub; depopulation and a collapse of the infrastructure would have made tourism in such regions a thing of the past.

CAP reform

The failure of the CAP to provide 'fair' incomes for the small farmers despite its vast cost has led to the universal recognition that reform is necessary. Unfortunately the true economic costs are difficult to quantify and seem to make little impact on politicians; they therefore base their decisions almost entirely upon the financial costs although these are of secondary importance. So reforms are aimed at reducing the budgetary costs without addressing the other ill effects of the policy. The undesirable consequences of the CAP largely result from high prices, but reducing them significantly is regarded as politically unacceptable and politicians therefore sought other ways of reducing budgetary costs. In 1984 a **quota system** was introduced for milk. This limited the support for milk production to a predetermined quota output, with extra production attracting a much lower price. This reduced the surpluses which must be disposed of (as butter) and hence the costs. However, it still left the consumers paying high prices and supporting producers via an implicit food tax.

For the first time, agricultural products were included in GATT interational trade negotiations which began in 1986. This Uruguay Round (where negotiations began) consequently put pressure on the Community to reform the CAP and 'major reforms', which turned out to be little more than tinkering, were agreed at the 1988 Fontainebleau European Council meeting. The reforms introduced the quota principle to some of the major crops as a **stabiliser system**. This sought to stabilise outputs and financial costs by reducing the prices of outputs which exceeded set thresholds (notice how words like 'stabilise' and 'threshold' were used instead of politically less acceptable words like 'limit' and 'quota'). In the event, the thresholds set were too generous and the price reductions for above-threshold production were too timid for the stabilizer system to have much impact on output or support costs. A voluntary 'set aside' system was also introduced. This offered a subsidy to farmers who agreed to take some of their land out of production, thus reducing output. The rewards offered were too low to be attractive to farmers, so again the impact on output was negligible.

Under increasing pressure from the Uruguay Round, Agricultural Commissioner Ray MacSharry made much more radical reform proposals in 1991(the **MacSharry reforms**). After months of angry debate a modified version was adopted by the Council of Ministers in May 1992. The pivotal change was a phased reduction in cereal prices to bring them 'close' to world prices by 1997, with compensatory **direct income payments** being paid to farmers (approximately the price reduction times the average historic yield in the locality times the number of hectares grown). To receive compensatory payments a farmer had to agree to set aside at least 15 per cent of the farm's arable area. Set aside land attracted a payment approximately equal to the profit foregone. Lower cereal prices imply reduced costs of animal feeds and the plan therefore included cuts in the prices of livestock products. (Except milk, for which the quota system was retained). The plan was remarkable because it attempted to replace politically manipulated prices with prices near to world market levels. How the set aside system offers large financial rewards to farmers who have the good

Fields that grow nothing yield lucrative harvest

FOR the past five years, Robert Sherriff and his wife Penny have been paid £27,000 a year for growing only grass on more than half their 600-acre farm. They will be paid as much as £42,000 this year.

Mr Sherriff is one of 35,000 arable farmers in Britain expected to apply for grants of up to £129 for every acre on which they do not plant crops. About 1.7 million acres, bigger than Lincolnshire, could be left fallow at a cost to the taxpayer of £200 million.

Faced with mounting food surpluses, Britain and other European Community states are paying farmers to grow nothing to counter years of paying them subsidies to grow too much.

The Sherriffs started harvesting cash rather than crops at Bayford, Hertfordshire, in 1988, when they volunteered with a few other pioneers for a five-year trial of the set-aside scheme. Since last year, set-aside has become virtually compulsory for arable farmers with more than 40 acres.

'I was attracted by the security of income,' Mr Sherriff said. 'There was a lot of talk in 1988 of agricultural reform and even of doing away with price support. Setaside offered a guaranteed £88 an acre for doing nothing except mow the grass once a year. About 150 acres of the farm had always been marginal, low-yielding land anyway.'

Mr Sherriff put down to grass 300 acres that had previously grown wheat, beans and oilseed rape. With half the farm idle, he laid off the two farmhands he had employed and hires contractors for such work as ploughing and spraying. Economists believe that at least one farming job is lost for every 300 acres set aside.

This year, under the even more generous compulsory scheme, Mr Sherriff is thinking of setting aside up to 375 acres. He will be entitled to £129 an acre for 60 per cent of this fallow area and £88 an acre for the rest, a total of about £42,000.

By taking part of his land out of production, he will qualify for other grants on the crops he does grow: £77 for each of his 170 acres of wheat and £144 for each of his 55 acres of beans, a further £21,000. The money is guaranteed even if his crops fail.

The Times, 21 March 1994

fortune to farm (or in this case *not* to farm) large areas of land is graphically set out in the box above. The move towards world prices was sufficient to enable the GATT negotiations to be concluded successfully in 1994 – after eight years of heated debate, and three years beyond the original deadline. The Community's acceptance of the MacSharry reforms, the first effective reform of the CAP to be agreed, was largely due to the overwhelming importance of trade to the EU.

With the prospect of further enlargement of the EU to include CEECs with large agricultural industries (see Chapters 8 and 9), further reforms to reduce price support costs have become urgent. So in

1999, Commissioner Fischler introduced further price reductions in the spirit of the MacSharry reforms (the **Fischler reforms**). Cereals prices are to be reduced through a 15% reduction in the intervention price. Again, compensatory direct income payments are to be made to farmers who agree to set aside at least 10% of the land previously used to grow cereals. The fall in cereal prices will reduce livestock feeding costs, so the price of beef is also set to fall. Here, market support is to fall by 20% with compensatory premium payments per animal. On environmental grounds, these premium payments are to be limited per hectare to discourage high stocking rates. The milk quota system was due to end in 2000, but has been extended until at least 2008. However, the quota is to be reduced by 2.4% and the intervention prices of butter and skimmed milk powder gradually reduced by 15%. As a result of these reforms, the EU's financial framework estimates for an EU of 21 expects agricultural budgetary costs of 45 billion in 2006 compared to 41 billion in 2000 for an EU of 15.

The MacSharry and Fischler reforms reduce internal market prices with compensatory direct income payments to farmers. The economic effects include lower food prices for consumers, with taxpayers providing the compensatory payments. This is a radical change because it transfers support costs from consumers to taxpayers. Also, lower agricultural prices and outputs permit a more rational allocation of resources within the EU. Similarly, the international allocation of resources will be ameliorated by a reduction in the quantity of EU surpluses being dumped on the world market. Does it make any difference if farmers get their incomes through artificially high prices or from a mix of lower prices and direct income payments? Yes, one reason is that agriculture produces two kinds of outputs. One type is marketed outputs, food mainly, the other is landscapes and wildlife. In the past farmers have received their incomes from the market only, with no rewards for environmental outputs, a clear case of **market failure**. Direct income payments will go some way towards correcting this, particularly if to qualify for them, farmers have to satisfy environmental requirements, such as reduced stocking rates.

The redistributive effects of the reformed CAP are more equitable in that poor consumers will no longer have to pay such high food prices to support farmers. However the benefits to farmers will still accrue largely to the richer farmers. In 1991 MacSharry proposed a ceiling on individual farmer receipts of the direct income payments which his plan was to introduce. The Conservative UK government complained that such an arrangement would discriminate against its larger and more efficient farmers – it did not publicly comment that such farmers were also amongst the more wealthy or that they usually voted for the then current government. Thus the UK persuaded the EU to miss an opportunity to achieve a more equitable distribution of incomes within farming.

Is the EU alone in providing generous support for its farmers? No, agricultural support is virtually universal. In its member countries, the Organisation for Economic Cooperation and Development, (OECD – the 'rich countries' club'), estimated that in 1999 about 40% of the value of farmers' receipts came from support. The figures for the USA are 25% and for Japan over 60%, with the corresponding EU figure being 50%. Clearly there is much for the Fischler reforms to achieve.

Conclusion

Until the early 1990s the EU avoided any significant reform of the CAP despite its obvious market-rigging folly, its vast expense and its failure to achieve its main income objective. However, the importance of trade to the EU turned out to be the lever which forced reform in the context of the **Uruguay Round of GATT trade negotiations**. Although output should in future be more subject to market forces, resource returns to land and farmers will still be subsidised, and the distribution of the gains within farming will still be mainly to the richer farmers.

KEY WORDS

Price elasticities	Green currencies
Economic efficiency	Agricultural Guarantee and
Target price	Guidance Fund
Variable import levy	Resource misallocation
Implicit food tax	Quota system
Intervention system	Stabiliser system
European Currency Units	MacSharry reforms
Monetary compensatory	Fischler reforms
amounts	GATT Uruguay Round

Further reading

Griffiths, A. and Wall, S. (eds). Chapter 28 in *Applied Economics* (8th edn). Pearson Education, 1999.

Romer, S. Chapter 7 in *Understanding the European Union* Anforme, 2000.

Sloman, J. Chapter 3 in *Economics* (4th edn). Pearson Education, 2000.

Useful websites

EU's agriculture website: www.europa.eu.int/comm/dg06/puli/index-en.htm
The United Nations Food and Agriculture Organisation: www.fao.org

Essay topics

1 (a) Explain how the Common Agricultural Policy attempts to maintain stable prices for agricultural products and ensure secure supplies for consumers in the European Union.
[12 marks]
  (b) Assess the view that the benefits of the Common Agricultural Policy outweigh the costs.
[13 marks]
  [AEB, Paper 2, Q5, January 1998.]
2 (a) Explain why it has been felt necessary to intervene in European agricultural markets.
[8 marks]
  (b) Comment on the effectiveness of the Common Agricultural Policy and discuss whether there is any need for further reforms.
[12 marks]
  [UCLES, Economics of Europe paper, Q3, March 1998.]

Data response question

The Common Agricultural Policy (CAP)

Article 39 of the Treaty of Rome called for the creation of a common policy for agriculture. The objectives of the policy were:

- to stabilize agricultural markets
- to raise agricultural productivity
- to increase farm income
- to assure the availability of supplies
- and to ensure reasonable prices for consumers

The CAP, adopted in the 1960s, was based on a system of price support backed up by variable import levies, intervention buying, export refunds and a structural policy. It is funded through the European Agricultural Guidance and Guarantee Fund (EAGGF).

During the 1980s concern about the economic and financial cost of the CAP mounted, both within and outside Europe. For example, between 1981 and 1991 total EAGGF expenditure increased by approximately 72% in real terms to almost 31 billion ECUs, 60% of the total EC budget. These concerns led to a series of measures to reform the CAP.

Figure 1 and Table 1 show the trends in agricultural prices and surpluses for selected agricultural commodities supported by the CAP.

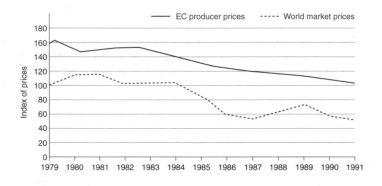

Figure 1 A comparison of EC producer prices[1] and world market prices[2] of agricultural commodities (1979–91), in real terms

Notes:

[1]EC producer price index = $\dfrac{\text{EC producer prices}}{\text{World market prices}}$

[2]World market price index in 1979 = 100

Table 1 Stocks of selected commodities held in EC intervention stores, thousand tonnes 1985/6–1990/1

Marketing year	Common wheat	Barley	All cereals	Butter	Skimmed- milk powder
1985/86	10 312	5296	18 502	1122	646
1986/87	7319	4235	14 271	1188	765
1987/88	4567	3916	11 748	640	240
1988/89	2906	3242	9146	64	7
1989/90	5521	3320	11 795	820	21
1990/91	8520	5538	18 729	324	354

(a) (i) Use Figure 1 to compare EC producer prices of agricultural commodities with world market prices from 1979 to 1991.

[2 marks]

(ii) Which commodity listed in Table 1 showed the greatest relative decline in intervention stocks between 1985/6 and 1988/9? [1 mark]

(b) (i) Explain **two** reasons why EC producer prices might be higher than world market prices. [4 marks]

(ii) Briefly explain the implications of CAP support for the world market prices of agricultural commodities. [3 marks]

(iii) Why might some countries outside the EC have benefited from the operation of the CAP and others suffered? [4 marks]

(c) Discuss whether price support is the best way of achieving the objectives of the CAP as set out in the Treaty of Rome. [6 marks]

[UCLES, Economics of Europe paper, Q1, June 1998.]

Chapter Five

Regional policy

The exploitation of comparative advantage may result in a regionally inequitable distribution of gains.

Chapters 2 and 3 dealt with the economic gains which were to flow from the introduction of free trade within Europe, both theoretically and in practice, particularly via the single market. Free trade permits efficiency and the maximisation of total income within the Union, but what about the distribution of that income? The effects on various groups – local, regional or national – may exacerbate existing inequalities. This chapter considers why the gains from the exploitation of comparative advantage may be distributed inequitably, and the consequent need for redistributive intervention. Regional policy should be seen as the first explicitly redistributive aspect of the EU. We now turn to the nature and causes of regional problems and the common policies designed to ameliorate them.

The nature and causes of regional problems
The major features of regional problems are relatively low incomes, low productivity and high unemployment, clearly these are inter-related. They are caused by a variety of **market imperfections.**

* Firstly, in the real world perfect mobility of factors or products does not exist. So locational factors become very important. These include access to large markets, access to inputs (raw materials, centres of administrative or financial expertise) and access to skilled labour.
* Secondly, comparing labour markets in different regions, wage differentials sometimes exceed productivity differences. Thus 'efficiency wages' (wages divided by productivity) can vary considerably, effectively rendering some regions uncompetitive.
* Thirdly, labour is not perfectly mobile. In practice the least skilled labour is least mobile. Conversely, the most skilled labour generally is mobile and leaves poor regions for employment in richer regions. These differences in labour mobilities exacerbate any initial regional income disparity.

A region may become depressed through some autonomous change in demand or supply or the interplay of market forces. In the EU context, comparative advantage benefits the more efficient firms, which expand their outputs and supplant the less efficient firms. Expansion and contraction are opposite sides of the same coin. Because of the market imperfections noted above, the gainers and losers from the single market tend to be regionally concentrated. A depressed region is unattractive to entrepreneurs and therefore lacks investment, so the depression becomes cumulative. There is no reason to expect market forces to correct regional imbalances. Regional income disparities are thus a form of **market failure** and government intervention is essential to their amelioration.

When one country becomes depressed relative to others with which it trades it is able to restore its competitiveness by depreciating its currency. Regions within a country are unable to help themselves to adjust in this fashion because they belong to a single currency nation. Each of the member states which are participating in monetary union (EMU, see Chapter 6) have adopted the Euro. They have a single currency, so each has lost the exchange rate method of overcoming a loss of competitiveness. Evidently, EMU emphasises the need for a regional policy.

In the early 1990s national income disparities were substantial. International comparisons of living standards are fraught with difficulty but comparisons of GDP per head in terms of '**purchasing power standards**' give a reasonably fair indication. On this basis the twelve richest members of the Union are reasonably close together, enjoying incomes significantly higher than those of the poorer three. In Greece GDP per head is about two thirds that of the average of the twelve. Portugal and Spain have GDPs per head which are about 74% and 80% respectively of the average of the twelve. The poorest regions of the poorer countries have average incomes which are only a quarter of those of the richest regions of the richer countries.

There are two main types of depressed region:

- First, rural areas where there is a heavy dependence upon agriculture, particularly if the farms are small leading to low labour productivity. Such areas are characterised by high unemployment and poorly developed infrastructures. The main low income agricultural regions are the south of Italy, most of Greece, much of Ireland and Portugal and large areas of Spain.
- Second, urban areas where traditional industries, such as coal mining, steel production, and ship building are declining. The depressed urban regions typically suffer high unemployment, decaying housing and infrastructures, and social deprivation. They

are found largely in Belgium, France, the eastern part of the unified Germany and the UK.

The evolution of regional policy

When the Union began in 1958 the original six members had their own different regional policies. Such national policies were generally intended to assist 'backward' regions, such as areas where traditional industries were in decline, to catch up with other areas. But at what level does assistance cease merely to compensate for regional disadvantages and become unfair national aids which distort competition? Clearly some Union-level policy coordination was necessary if competitive forces were not to be negated, but in practice, so long as the Union enjoyed rapid economic growth and high overall employment these issues were left to member states. Common policy was restricted to the establishment of the European Investment Bank (EIB). This was called for by Article 3 of the Treaty of Rome, largely with the south of Italy, the Mezzogiorno, in mind as the only major relatively poor area in the original six countries. The same Article called for the establishment of a European Social Fund (some aspects of social policy are discussed in Chapter 3). The ESF dealt with employment issues, particularly the retraining of workers displaced by structural change, leaving the main areas of social policy such as health, education, housing and pensions, to national authorities. EIB expenditures were, and still are, concentrated on improvements to infrastructures (improved roads, water supplies, etc.) in the poorer regions. The complementary nature of the expenditures of the ESF in these regions to improve working conditions and provide training – in short to raise labour productivity – make the Social Fund a part of regional policy.

In the early days of the CAP, its price supporting activities were also thought of as having a regional role, in raising incomes in poor agricultural regions. As discussed in Chapter 4, the CAP tended in practice to favour the richer farmers in the richer regions and its price-distorting activities have been of little benefit in reducing regional income disparities. However the Guidance Section of EAGGF does have a regional role and its assistance has been focused on the poorer agricultural regions. Guidance Section expenditure is now considered to be part of the regional structural funds.

The coincidence of EU enlargement problems, a reduction in the rate of economic growth and global depression in the mid-1970s increased general unemployment and left few opportunities for unemployed workers in poorer areas. Regional problems were thus

Table 7 Expenditures of the structural funds, 1994–98 (million Ecu)

	1994	1995	1996	1997	1998
EAGGF Guidance Section	2533	2531	3360	3580	3522
Financial Instrument for Fisheries Guidance	395	248	422	487	408
European Regional Development Fund	6331	8374	10610	11521	11797
European Social Fund	4333	4547	6032	6143	7603
Cohesion Fund	852	1699	1872	2323	2449
Other	1623	1647	2163	1994	2774
Totals	16067	19046	24459	26048	28553

Source: EU Financial Report 1998.

highlighted resulting in the establishment of the **European Regional Development Fund** (ERDF) in 1975. This was particularly welcomed by the UK, which saw a regional policy as a means of obtaining some redistributive benefits to help in offsetting the large budgetary transfers resulting from CAP arrangements. ERDF expenditure is supposed to be matched by governmental expenditure and be subject to 'additionality', that is, its expenditures should be in addition to, not instead of, normal government expenditures – a point which UK governments, in the past, tended to ignore.

The accession of Greece in 1981 and Portugal and Spain in 1986, all relatively poor countries, increased the importance of regional policies and EU expenditures increased substantially as shown in Tables 6 and 7. At the same time the Single European Act envisaged the introduction of the single market which might increase existing regional disparities. Accordingly the SEA formally recognised the importance of regional redistribution and called for the coordination of existing policies and increased funding. The ERDF, ESF and the Guidance Section of EAGGF were grouped together as the **structural funds** whose activities were to be coordinated

The expanding importance of regional policy

In 1988 the European Council decided to double in real terms the resources devoted to structural funds over the next five years, and to give priority to regions where GDP per head was less than 75% of the EU average. The TEU expanded the policy further, creating a **Committee of**

Regions as well as the **Cohesion Fund**. The latter is to help countries where the GNP is less than 90 per cent of the EU average – Greece, Ireland, Portugal and Spain. Beginning operations in 1993 it focuses on improvements to infrastructures, particularly the trans-European networks in transport and energy. The Cohesion Fund is thus another structural fund. One of its main aims is to aid the poorer countries to meet the 'convergence criteria'; thus there is an explicit link to economic and monetary union. With the latter's removal of monetary and exchange rate policies from national governments, whole member states, unable to adjust to changing economic circumstances, could become 'poorer regions'. Regional policy may thus become a major element of redistributive policies required to compensate for the inequitable distribution of incomes which the free market could generate.

Yet another structural fund was added to the list in 1993, the Financial Instrument for Fisheries Guidance, as further major increases in resources began, with the structural funds set to reach 35% of total EU expenditure by 1999. The rapid increase in expenditures by the structural funds in total during the 1990s is shown by Table 6 in the previous chapter. In table 7 the expenditure is broken down by fund for the years 1994-98.

In addition to the expenditures of the structural funds national governments have been able to use the EIB to finance development and infrastructure investments at the lowest available interest rates. In 1999 the EIB loaned ∈ 27.8 billions, a sum almost equal to the structural funds' expenditure.

How does regional policy work?
At the beginning of this chapter the major problems were diagnosed as being poor location with respect to markets (i.e. high transport costs), industrial decline, low labour productivity, and unemployment. Accordingly, the policy framework for the structural funds listed the following six objectives:

- to help regions lagging behind in their development, i.e. having GDP per capita less than 75% of EU average
- to aid regions suffering industrial decline
- to combat unemployment, especially long term, of the young and of the excluded
- to help workforces to adjust to industrial change
- (a) to help with the improvement of agricultural and fisheries structures; and (b) to develop rural areas in difficult circumstances

Table 8 2000–06 Planned structural fund expenditures (∈ million; 1999 prices)

	1	Transitional support objective 1	2	Transitional support objective 2	3	FIFG	Total
				Objectives			
Belgium	0	625	368	65	737	34	1029
Denmark	0	0	156	27	365	197	745
Germany	19229	729	2984	526	4581	107	28156
Greece	20961	0	0	0	0	0	20961
Spain	37744	352	2553	98	2140	200	43087
France	3254	551	5437	613	4540	225	14620
Ireland	1315	1773	0	0	0	0	3088
Italy	21935	187	2145	377	3744	96	28484
Luxembourg	0	0	34	6	38	0	78
Netherlands	0	123	676	119	1686	31	2635
Austria	261	0	578	102	528	4	1473
Portugal	16124	2905	0	0	0	0	19029
Finland	913	0	459	30	403	31	1836
Sweden	722	0	354	52	720	60	1908
United Kingdom	5085	1166	3989	706	4568	121	15635
Total EU15	**127543**	**8411**	**19733**	**2721**	**24050**	**1106**	**183564**

Source: 11th Annual Report on the Structural Funds, COM(2000)698 Final.

- to aid regions with low population densities (Finland and Sweden only).

The total funds available were shared out amongst the member states according to their plans to achieve these objectives. In the period 2000–06 these objectives have been simplified under three heads. Objective 1 is still to help regions lagging behind in their development, together with the Finnish and Swedish regions of low population density. Objective 2 is for regions in industrial decline, while objective 3 will support education, training and employment. Table 8 gives the planned expenditures 2000–06 under the revised framework. The transitional support columns relate to the continuation of pre-existing projects under 'old' objectives 1 and 2 which are gradually being phased out, such as some of the remote areas of Scotland. The UK planned expenditures noted in the table are focused on South Yorkshire, West Wales and the Valleys, Cornwall, the Scilly Isles and Merseyside.

Conclusions

Regional policy has its origins in the need to assist the poorer regions, both rural areas heavily dependent on small farms and urban areas with a concentration of declining industries. As European integration proceeds the gains from the exploitation of comparative advantage tend to benefit some regions more than others, indeed the decline of some areas may be accelerated. Consequently redistributive regional policies are increasingly important. By 1992 such structural policies already accounted for one quarter of the EU budget, and increased to 35% in 1999, at which level it is intended to remain during the 2000-06 period. The poorer EU regions and states are benefiting from a substantial transfer of resources. The further integration represented by economic and monetary union, examined in the next chapter, together with further enlargements discussed in Chapter 9, will underline the importance of the role of regional and other redistributive policies.

KEY WORDS

Market failure	Committee of Regions
Structural funds	Cohesion Fund

Further reading

Anderton, A. Unit 38 in *Economics* (3rd edn). Causeway Press, 2000.
Griffiths, A. and Wall, S. (eds). Chapter 11 in *Applied Economics*, (8th edn). Pearson Education, 1999.
Smith, D. Chapter 8 in *UK Current Economic Policy* (2nd edn). Heinemann Educational, 1999.

Useful website

EU's regional policy: www.europa.eu.int/comm/dg16/

Essay topics

1. (a) Explain why the EU operates a regional policy.   [10 marks]
   (b) Discuss the implications of the proposed enlargement of the EU on the operation of the area's regional policy.   [15 marks]
2. (a) Discuss the main objectives of the EU's regional policy.
                                                            [10 marks]
   (b) Evaluate the effectiveness of the EU's regional policy.
                                                            [15 marks]

Data response question

Regions placed in the lower half of EU rankings of productivity

London is the only area of Britain in the top 34 European Union regions in terms of economic performance measured by productivity and gross domestic product per head, according to the latest survey from Business Strategies, the employment analyst. It argues that, although the UK's regions have seen a sustained improvement in the growth of their employment rates since 1995, this was not paralleled with a similar expansion in productivity performance. The net growth in Britain's flexible labour markets has been in lower paid, less quality based jobs not through an increase in higher value-added industries ...

The British capital is ranked eighth in the overall table, well behind Hamburg in Germany, which lies far ahead in gross domestic product per head although in second place behind Brussels when it comes to productivity achievement ...

The survey found that, while UK regional employment rates were higher than elsewhere in western Europe, with all 12 of the country's regions being in the top half of the 170 EU rankings, all the UK regions fell into the lower half of EU productivity rankings except for London.

Source: extracts from 'Regions placed in lower half of EU rankings of productivity' by Robert Taylor, *Financial Times*, 24/11/00.

(a) (i) Explain what is meant by productivity. [2 marks]
   (ii) Identify two features of regional problems other than low productivity. [2 marks]
(b) According to the survey from Business Strategies, how did the performance of UK regions compare to those of regions in other EU countries? [6 marks]
(c) Discuss two reasons why regional differences exist. [4 marks]
(d) Explain why, in recent decades, the EU has increased its expenditure on regional policy. [6 marks]

Chapter Six
Economic and monetary union

One market ... one money

Economic and monetary union is the final stage in economic integration, it alone will enable the EU to capture *all* of the benefits of the single market. It means the replacement of national currencies with a single European currency and centralized control of monetary and economic policies. *It involves such a pooling of sovereignty that some form of political union is the only logical conclusion.*

The EMU debate
There is a limit to the degree of market integration which can be achieved so long as national currencies and economic policies exist. Even in the absence of tariff barriers, and if all technical standards and company laws were harmonized and all non-tariff barriers removed, national currencies would still inhibit competition. They do this in two ways. First, the conversion of one currency into another adds to costs. Second, the possibility that the exchange rates between currencies may change during a deal adds substantially to uncertainty. These uncertainties are magnified by differences in inflation rates. Finally, different economic policies in member states result in different rates of interest and different methods and rates of taxation both for companies and consumers. It follows that the full benefits of the internal market can only be achieved by full economic and monetary union.

Brief mention should be made here of the CAP. One of its problems has been that of uncommon prices caused by the 'green' currency exchange rate system. A common currency would resolve this difficulty and ease the operation of the CAP either in its old or reformed state.

What is the economic case against EMU?
Take the case of a member country with balance of payments problems causing its exchange rate to fall. It has three policy options:

- using its reserves of gold and foreign currency to support its desired exchange rate
- raising its interest rate to increase the international demand for its currency

- curing the underlying problem. For example, it may be that a high inflation rate is making the country uncompetitive and anti-inflationary policies are required.

Any or all of these policies may fail, and then equilibrium must be restored by altering the exchange rate, or permitting it to be determined by market forces. If the country in question is locked into an EMU, it possesses none of these options – its currency is the common currency, fixed in terms of its partners – it has the same rate of inflation as its partners. So if its workers demand higher wages and fail to increase productivity accordingly they will become unemployed; national economic policy has no power beyond that of persuasion to help them.

In reality these arguments against EMU are political in that control over economic policy instruments is lost by individual countries. This loss of control is indeed very substantial. The possibility of one country becoming depressed relative to the others implies corrective action involving considerable resource transfers; ultimately redistributive regional policies as part of a central budget and some form of central economic policy coordination would be essential.

Evidently the EMU debate turns out to be political as well as economic, and the present discussion must avoid taking sides and concentrate on the economic issues. These deal with how EMU may be achieved, and chart developments.

How can EMU be achieved?

There are three essential elements to EMU:

- a single currency
- an EU central bank
- the coordination of EU economic policy.

A single currency, the first hurdle, is the one which appears to attract most attention – not surprisingly, for once this has been agreed the other elements of EMU must follow.

The transition towards EMU would be very disruptive if economic conditions between member states differed much when a single currency was introduced. Consequently detailed **convergence criteria** were agreed. They were set out in the TEU, and continued the general direction of **cohesion policy** followed since EMU was called for in the Single European Act. Each member state must satisfy the criteria before joining the EMU. The criteria related to:

- price stability
- favourable interest rates
- stable exchange rates
- reasonable level of government debt.

Price stability was defined as an annual rate of inflation which was no more than 1.5 per cent above that of the average of the three best performing member states. A favourable interest rate was similarly defined except that the permitted maximum difference was 2 per cent. A stable exchange rate meant keeping within a 2.25% ERM band (discussed below) for at least two years. Finally, government debt must be no more than 60 per cent of GDP. We now turn to the common co-operative attempt to stabilise exchange rates.

The European Monetary System (EMS)

The EMS was introduced in 1979 with both short- and long-term aims. The short-term aim was to stabilise exchange rates, which in turn would help to stabilise prices, and foster internal trade. The need for exchange rate stabilisation was underlined by fluctuations in international exchange rates, notably those involving the dollar. If the dollar fell in value, speculators immediately moved funds into European currencies, but favoured some more than others. Thus within Europe, relative exchange rates would be distorted – changing away from the levels justified by relative market conditions. The long-term aim was to increase economic convergence as an essential element of the ultimate move towards EMU.

As part of the EMS each member state (including the UK) handed 20 per cent of its gold and foreign currency reserves to the **European Monetary Cooperation Fund** in return for ECUs (discussed below). These could be used in transactions within the EU. The ECU (**European Currency Unit**) was introduced (replacing the very similar European Unit of Account) as a composite currency; i.e. it was a unit based on a 'weighted basket' of members' currencies. The weight assigned to each currency was proportional to the relative size of that country's economy. As the largest economy, Germany's mark had the largest weight in the ECU. The composition of the ECU was reviewed every few years, but it was fixed when the TEU came into force as shown in Table 9.

The Exchange Rate Mechanism (ERM) was the central part of the EMS and its operation was intended to provide exchange rate stability. The currency of each member had a specific value (parity) in terms of the ECU. In turn this meant that each currency had a parity value in

Table 9 Composition of the Ecu in 1996

Currency	Percentage weights
Belgian franc	7.8
Danish krone	2.5
German mark	30.5
Greek drachma	0.8
Spanish peseta	5.2
French franc	19.4
Irish punt	1.1
Italian lira	9.9
Luxembourg franc	0.3
Dutch guilder	9.5
Portugese escudo	0.8
British pound	12.1
Total	100.00

Source: Europe in the Round 1996-7 CD ROM

terms of each of the other member currencies. When the ERM began any one currency was permitted to vary by plus or minus 2.25 per cent against any other member currency. When this margin was reached the two central banks concerned had to intervene to keep within the limits. There was a second element to the mechanism, a divergence indicator, which was three-quarters of a country's permitted variation against the Ecu. When this indicator was reached the country was expected to take corrective action. Thus if the currency fell in value the government might increase interest rates, increase taxation or support the currency.

By 1989 only the three poorest southern European member states – Greece, Portugal and Spain – together with the UK, had not joined the ERM. The three intended to join as soon as their economic circumstances permitted, Spain did so in 1989 and Portugal in 1992, both with 6 per cent permitted bands of variation against their central parity. In the UK, political opposition to the ERM, because it was seen as yet another sacrifice of sovereignty, militated against joining. However against the will of many on the right of the government the UK joined in October 1990. The sterling exchange rate at which the UK chose to join was regarded by many as too high, a subject which is discussed in Chapter 10.

Appraisal of the EMS

The main objectives of the EMS are economic convergence and exchange rate stability, important prerequisites for economic and monetary union.

Real convergence is the convergence of EU economies to the highest current EU living standards through the catching up of the poorer countries and regions. The EMS could not directly cause this convergence but it could help to produce the stable economic environment in which real convergence could occur, helped by the cohesion policy.

Nominal convergence implies convergence towards the lowest rates of inflation, and to balance of payments and budget balances which together encourage more stable exchange rates – the ideal prelude to EMU is exchange rates which are so stable that they can be fixed, and replaced with a single currency.

Between 1979 and 1992 inflation rates gradually converged and fell, helping substantially to stabilise exchanges rates. The latter enjoyed stability but not rigidity: over the period there were 12 realignments agreed quietly and collectively rather than with the dramas previously associated with such changes. The stability was intra-EC, of course fluctuations of the ECU against external currencies

Speculators humiliate ERM

Currency speculators and international investors celebrated victory over the European Community yesterday, as weak currencies in the now defunct European exchange rate mechanism were savaged and Germany was angrily blamed for the system's collapse.

European politicians said Germany had failed to respect its obligations in the ERM and had triggered its death. The European Commission warned that the dismantling of the ERM and its economic consequences threatened to put countries at each others' throats and wreck the single market.

The ERM was pronounced all but dead after the meeting of finance ministers and central bank governors broke up early on Monday morning. They let all currencies apart from the German mark and Dutch guilder fluctuate by up to 15 per cent from their central rate. Economists said the widening of the bands was purely cosmetic and that Europe had re-adopted a system of floating exchange rates after 14 years in which the ERM had been the cornerstone of European economic cooperation.

Robert Chote and Andrew Marshall, *The Independent*, 3 August 1993

were not affected. The ERM began to be considered very successful, and was joined in 1989 by Spain, in 1990 by the UK (at what was generally considered too high a rate, see Chapter 10) and finally in 1992 by Portugal. The rate of inflation in Greece was too high for ERM membership.

A major reason for falling inflation rates prior to 1992 was that participation in the ERM was a constraint on domestic policies. Budget deficits were less easily cured by devaluations. Capital controls and the manipulation of short-term interest rates were the methods used to keep exchange rates within their set limits. However the liberalisation of capital movements under the Single Market Programme, the reunification of Germany and the decision to proceed to EMU coincided to help destabilise the system. To meet the Maastricht criteria for EMU, countries had to reduce budget deficits at a time when the Community was moving into recession. An inflationary German budget deficit caused by reunification resulted in the Bundesbank raising interest rates to relatively high levels. The German mark increased in value, and to keep their exchange rates within the agreed limits in a system where the Ecu was dominated by the DM, other countries were forced to raise their interest rates. EU recession and unemployment increased but interest rates were maintained.

In the context of the single market programme's freeing of capital movements, the ERM turned out to have a major flaw so far as speculation is concerned. Currencies were locked into it with only narrow bands of exchange rate variation permitted. So if changes in one country made its exchange rate appear unsustainable, speculators could move huge quantities of capital in the expectation of a change in the currency, with little risk of serious losses but hopes of major gains. Had the exchange rate not been locked into a narrow band, its gradual devaluation would have limited the profits and therefore the motivation for speculation, but the prospect of a large change increased speculative pressures. So, late in 1992 speculators decided that some exchange rates were unsustainable and massive transfers of funds forced both the lira and pound out of the ERM in September. Continued speculation during the following months forced several currencies to devalue. Eventually, intense speculation resulted in the ERM bands being widened to 15% in August 1993. In the accompanying boxed article from *The Independent* the ERM is pronounced 'all but dead'.

The announcement of the death of the ERM turned out to be premature. Soon, Germany began to cut its interest rates and stability began to return. The wide bands increased flexibility, reduced the likelihood of speculation and nine countries remained within the ERM. Although the wide bands were retained, the nine gradually returned to the old narrow bands in practice. In 1995 Austria joined the ERM followed in 1996 by Finland and Italy.

Table 10 provides the inflation rate background to the changes discussed. The 1985 and 1990 data illustrate the general reduction in inflation during the first stable period, although German inflation is seen to have increased due to reunification. After the exchange rate storms of 1992–3 stability returned, with inflation rates again converging on their downward paths.

The EMU agreement at Maastricht

After much debate, the European Council agreed to permit the introduction of the single currency in countries which met the following convergence criteria:

- an inflation rate no more than 1.5% above the average of the three members with the lowest inflation rates
- long-term interest rates less than 2% above those of the three members with the lowest inflation rates
- budget deficit less than 3% of GDP
- government debt less than 60% of GDP
- stable currency – having stayed within 2.25% of its ERM parity value for two years.

Table 10 Rates of inflation in the EU selected years

	1985	1990	1995	1996	1997	1998
Belgium	5.9	3.5	1.5	2.0	1.3	1.6
Denmark	4.3	2.7	1.8	1.8	1.8	2.1
Germany	1.8	2.8	2.0	1.6	0.8	1.0
Greece	18.3	19.9	9.3	8.3	6.7	4.9
Spain	7.1	6.5	4.6	3.6	2.1	2.3
France	5.8	2.8	1.6	1.8	1.4	0.9
Ireland	5.1	2.0	2.5	2.3	3.5	5.6
Italy	9.0	5.9	5.8	4.1	2.6	2.8
Luxembourg	4.3	5.5	2.0	1.7	3.3	1.5
Netherlands	2.4	2.2	1.1	1.9	2.0	1.9
Austria	3.3	3.3	2.2	2.1	1.6	0.6
Portugal	19.4	11.6	4.2	3.1	2.7	4.1
Finland	5.6	6.0	1.1	1.0	2.1	2.9
Sweden	6.9	9.6	2.7	1.7	1.2	1.3
United Kingdom	5.3	5.5	2.6	2.7	2.9	3.2

Source: *European Economy 69,* 1999.

There was to be some coordination of economic policies, but taxation was to remain in the hands of member governments. Agreeing maximum levels of budget deficits and debts was necessary because a government might otherwise run up huge debts, denominated in the single currency, and then expect to be 'bailed out' by the EU. The agreement makes it clear that this will not happen, indeed the offending government may be fined for its transgression. Of course there are situations where a bigger budget deficit may be desirable, for example if an external shock such as an oil price rise, affected one country more than others, causing major unemployment. In such circumstances the EU may decide not to impose a fine, but in the long term the member would still be expected to impose its own fiscal discipline.

The timetable
The European Council adopted a three stage timetable. **Stage One** began in July 1990. During this stage the aim was to encourage further economic convergence, price stability, and sound public finance. The cohesion policy designed to raise the economic circumstances of the poorer Union members towards those of the richer members – discussed in the previous chapter – was a major element. As agreed in the TEU **Stage Two** began on 1 January 1994 with the establishment of the **European Monetary Institute** (EMI) as the precursor of a

future European Central Bank. The EMI aimed to increase cooperation between members' central banks – all of which had to become independent of government, to coordinate their monetary policies, to encourage the convergence of inflation and interest rates, and help to stabilise exchange rates. *These duties of the EMI could be summarised as guiding member states towards the attainment of the convergence criteria which are fundamental to a smooth transition to EMU.*

Stage Three is economic and monetary union for those members meeting the criteria and wishing to proceed to full economic and monetary union, leaving the other members outside the new union until they have caught up, their position being reviewed every two years. In the event, eleven members adopted the single currency on 1st January 1999, leaving four countries outside the system: Denmark, Greece, Sweden and the UK.

The EMI has been transmuted into the **European Central Bank** (ECB), and the exchange rates of participating members are irrevocably fixed in terms of the **Euro** ($\in$)- the new name of the Ecu. National currencies are to co-exist with the Euro until 2002 when only the Euro will be legal tender. The ECB is independent of the Commission, the European Parliament and national governments. It defines and executes EU monetary policy, undertakes its foreign exchange operations, holds its foreign reserves, and is the sole authoriser of notes and coin, although these may be issued by national central banks.

Clearly EMU involves huge changes in sovereignty. Those against

---

GORDON BROWN'S 5 ECONOMIC TESTS

In October 1997 the Chancellor of the Exchequer, Gordon Brown, set out the Labour Government's criteria for recommending membership of the euro.

These criteria are described as the five economic tests and are that membership must:

- promote employment, prosperity and economic growth
- be beneficial to the UK's financial services
- encourage inward direct foreign investment
- allow sufficient flexibility to deal with economic change and demand- and supply-side shocks
- occur when there is sufficient convergence between UK economic activity and the economic activity of the current members.

EMU describe it as an unacceptable loss of national sovereignty, those in favour consider it to be an essential pooling of sovereignty. All EU members signed and ratified the TEU and so presumably agree with its ultimate destination. Well, most members agree. The UK ratified the treaty despite expressing public doubts and insisted on a protocol leaving the final decision on joining the EMU to a future government and parliament. However, the new Labour government has a radically different attitude to the previous Conservatives and seems to favour joining if and when the circumstances are right (see the boxed item 'Gordon Brown's 5 Economic Tests'). Denmark also had mixed feelings and agreed an opt-out. In both countries the final decisions are likely to be taken in national referenda. Greece joined the EMU on 1st January 2001 (see the boxed item below).

What is the relationship between those inside the EMU and those outside? Suppose the outside countries devalued their currencies against the Euro, an action which might be seen as unfair by EMU countries. Some Euro-zone members might then want to take retalia-

Greece steps up to join the euro club of nations

Europe's oldest currency will today cease to exist when Greece becomes the twelfth member of European economic and monetary union (EMU).

The drachma, believed to have first been minted in about 650 BC finished trading on the financial markets last Friday and will from today be absorbed into the euro. Greek financial institutions will begin trading in euros on Wednesday when they reopen for business after an extended new year break.

Greece's entry into the eurozone follows a substantial economic overhaul triggered when its initial application to join the currency at launch was rejected. But despite an austerity programme which has seen public spending tumble, Greece's stock of debt still exceeds its national income – far above the 60 per cent debt to GDP ratio laid down in the Maastricht Treaty.

'The admission of Greece into the eurozone is, simultaneously, an adventure, a challenge and a chance for this country,' said Marios Camhis, the Athens representative of the European Commission. 'Greece has to be vigilant that it does not lose its pace because inflation and deficits can return.'

Wim Duisenberg, President of the European Central Bank (ECB), said 'I think we have to say that Greece has made great and commendable efforts to reach this stage. It still has to undertake great efforts to make the position it had reached upon entry a sustainable one.'

Source: *The Times*, 1 January 2001.

tory action such as the introduction of countervailing tariffs. Clearly this would damage the single market. Such problems have been allowed for in the introduction of a new ERM on a voluntary basis. In essence this suggests that the outside members should restrict their currency movements to a 15% band either side of their parity values with the Euro.

Conclusion

These topics clearly raise both political and economic issues which must be kept apart in the mind of the economist. On the economic benefits of EMU an empirical study, *One Market, One Money,* published in November 1990 by the Commission (with the support and advice of several economists outside the Commission) produced some interesting conclusions. It expected EMU to reduce the rate of inflation, and since there would be one currency only, exchange rate transactions costs would be removed. Both of these factors would contribute to a significant reduction in uncertainty and so encourage an expansion in investment. The consequent increase in Union GDP would be of the order of 6 per cent and dynamic in nature – that is approximately equal to the expected economic benefits of the single market discussed in Chapter 2. It is too soon to begin asking if EMU is a success.

KEY WORDS

Convergence
European Monetary System
  (EMS)
European Currency Unit (Ecu;
  becomes the Euro)

Exchange Rate Mechanism
  (ERM)
European Monetary Institute
  (EMI)
European Central Bank (ECB)

Further reading

Bamford, C. and Grant, S. Chapter 5 in *The UK Economy in a Global Context*. Heinemann Educational, 2000.

Russell, M. and Heathfield, D. Chapter 10 in *Inflation and UK Monetary Policy* (3rd edn). Heinemann Educational, 1999.

Smith, D. Chapter 9 in *UK Current Economic Policy* (2nd edn). Heinemann Educational, 1999.

Useful websites

European Central Bank: www.ecb.int/
EU's site on EMU: www.europa.eu.int/

Essay topics

1. (a) Examine two ways in which joining a monetary union imposes constraints on the UK's macroeconomic policy options.
   [40 marks]
   (b) Examine the benefits to a country of being a member of a monetary union.   [60 marks]
   [Edexcel, Unit Test 6 Specimen Paper, Q1, 2000.]
2. (a) Explain the benefits which are likely to result from specialisation and trade.   [12 marks]
   (b) Discuss whether the adoption of a single European currency by the United Kingdom would improve or damage the performance of the United Kingdom economy.   [13 marks]
   [AEB, Paper 2, Q10, Summer 1998.]

Data response question

The Pros and Cons on entry into the EMU

Britain would receive three undeniable advantages from joining the EMU. British travellers would save money on currency exchanges. Exporters would no longer have to hedge exchange rates. And investors, including industrial investors in Britain, could compare investment opportunities in Britain and Europe without having to worry about currency risks or the complex financial strategies required to keep them under control ...

Three significant economic drawbacks of EMU are slightly more complex, but equally undeniable. First, British interest rates would no longer be set by British officials to manage economic conditions in Britain. Nor would British voters be able to determine the objectives of economic policy. Specifically, British politicians and voters would lose all say in the difficult decisions that inevitably have to be made about the short-term trade-offs between inflation and unemployment ...

Secondly, the exchange rate would no longer balance Britain's trade and capital flows with the rest of the world. Fixing the exchange rate does not somehow 'fix' the econ-

omy's need to adjust to constantly changing business conditions at home and abroad ... Fixing the exchange rate simply shifts uncertainty from the currency to another economic parameter, such as inflation, the rate of interest, the level of taxes or the length of the dole queues and the state of economic demand ...

The third undeniable economic disadvantage is equally subtle. Even if membership of the single currency were desirable in the long run, it would be impossible – from a purely economic standpoint – to decide on the 'right' exchange rate at which to join ...

Ireland joined EMU at an exchange rate that was much too weak. It is therefore experiencing socially disruptive levels of inflation, especially in housing.

Source: extracts from 'Economics really has little to do with euro decision' by Anatole Kaletsky, *The Times*, 5/9/00.

(a) (i)   Define EMU.   [2 marks]
     (ii) Explain one advantage Britain would gain from joining the EMU.   [2 marks]
(b) Discuss why an interest rate set by the ECB may not be beneficial for the British economy.   [4 marks]
(c) Explain why a fixed exchange rate 'simply shifts uncertainty from the currency to another economic parameter'.   [6 marks]
(d) Discuss the likely effects of joining EMU at an exchange rate that is too strong.   [6 marks]

Chapter Seven
Globalisation

... interdependence recreates the world in the image of a global village.' The Gutenberg Galaxy (1962) Marshall McLuhan

When the Common Market began, the centrepiece was the common external tariff, and the gains to be achieved from exploiting comparative advantage within the Community, as discussed in Chapter 2. The full benefits could only be achieved in a market free from all barriers, not just tariff barriers, and Chapter 3 examined how the Single European Act sought to introduce the Single Market. Now, through international trade negotiations, trade barriers have become very low, and the gains from **comparative advantage** have become more available globally. This chapter begins by examining the position of the EU in world trade and the liberalisation of international trade. It then considers the resulting **globalisation** and its consequences.

Even excluding intra-EU trade, which accounts for over 60% of members states' trade, the EU is one of the world's major traders, and the largest exporter, as Table 11 shows. So in addition to the liberalisation of trade within Europe, it has a major stake in the reduction of trade barriers internationally.

Liberalisation of international trade

In 1947 the leading trading nations signed the **General Agreement on Tariffs and Trade** (GATT). This sought to avoid the protectionism of the 1930s which had greatly exacerbated the worldwide 'Great

Table 11 Share of EU in world trade 1999

	Imports (%)	Exports(%)
EU	18.5	19.5
USA	24.6	17.0
Japan	7.2	10.1
China	8.1	8.9
Russia	0.9	1.8
Others	40.7	42.7

Sources: derived from *Monthly Bulletin of Statistics*, United Nations, and *Eurostat Yearbook* 2000.

Depression'. Its main aim was to reduce trade barriers, though it excluded agriculture and services. Its crucial principle is the **most-favoured-nation** clause; under this, a country agreeing a tariff reduction to one country is obliged to offer the same reduction to all GATT members. How can the EU countries with zero internal tariffs and a common external tariff against third countries belong to GATT? The latter's rules exempt customs unions and free trade areas from this non-discrimination rule, provided that their formation does not raise the tariffs of the new trade group to a level greater on average than the previous tariffs of the individual members. It is also permissible to offer reduced tariffs on a discriminatory basis to developing countries.

In Article 110 of the Treaty of Rome the Community states its intention of contributing to 'the harmonious development of world trade, the progressive abolition of restrictions on international exchanges and the lowering of customs barriers'. To date, the Community has three main discriminatory agreements: two are for reciprocal free trade in industrial products with the European Free Trade Area and ten Central and East European Countries (see Chapter 8); the other – the **Lomé Convention** – offers non-reciprocal tariff preferences for most non-agricultural goods and preferential access for some food products. The Lomé Convention covers 66 African, Caribbean and Pacific (ACP) countries, mostly the ex-colonies of EU members. In addition to trade preferences it also provides aid for the ACP countries with special funds to stabilize their export earnings, and a European Development Fund to finance development projects.

From time to time GATT members enter a round of international negotiations to try to liberalize trade. As the EU has a common trade policy the Commission represents it, though its agreements have to be ratified by the Council of Ministers. Successive rounds of negotiations in GATT since 1947 give the impression that trade barriers have been progressively reduced since tariffs have certainly fallen to low levels. The truth is that their place was taken by NTBs. Two examples underline the point. The Multi-fibre Arrangements (between developed-country textile importers, notably EU, USA and Japan, and developing-country exporters) placed quantitative restrictions on trade. Similarly, the EU's large trade deficit with Japan led to the imposition of Voluntary Export Restraints (VERs) on a wide range of goods such as cars and electronic items. Such quantitative restrictions became common. In 1985 it was agreed to launch a new round of trade negotiations, the **Uruguay Round** (since this is where the initial conference was held), to be completed by the end of 1990. As this round was to include agriculture in addition to tariffs and NTBs, it is not surprising that progress was slow. The main protagonists were the USA and the EU. The former is the world's major food exporter and had to compete in world markets with heavily subsidized European food exports. So the USA wanted to see the EU's agricultural policy remodelled to remove these dumped surpluses and offered to reform its own system of protecting agriculture. In the event, GATT negotiations ground on and on, not producing a new agreement until December 1993, almost three years beyond the original deadline. As discussed in Chapter 4, major agricultural concessions testify to the importance of trade to the EU.

In 1995 the name of GATT was changed to the World Trade Organisation (WTO). Its role, methods and existing trade agreements remained unchanged. The remainder of this chapter will look at the extent of globalisation, including foreign direct investment (FDI), discuss why it is happening, and try to assess the consequences.

After the Uruguay GATT round, the reduction in trade barriers stimulated increased trade flows. Between 1988 and 1998 world trade in goods (defined as the real value of the sum of merchandise exports and imports) increased from 21.2% of GDP to 28.3% of GDP. For high income countries the increases are much greater, rising from 28.3% to 38.3% of GDP. The EU is the world's largest trading area and its trade with the rest of the world increased from 41% to 54.4% of GDP (World Bank, 2000 World Development Indicators).

As trade barriers became negligible, product, capital and services markets became increasingly integrated on a global scale. In the EU, trade in services is now about one third of the value of merchandise trade. Services includes transport, particularly air and sea, insurance and other financial services, royalties, and increasingly, communications related activities.

Investment flows are the other major element of trade. Private capital flows representing investments overseas have long been important to European and other economies, and FDI has grown rapidly over the last decade. Quoting net figures of investment flows suggests little is happening because inward flows and outward flows tend to cancel each other. However, if inward and outward flows are summed, the resulting gross figures better demonstrate their significance. Gross private capital flows (sum of inward and outward flows), in real terms, increased from 6.9% to 14.5% of world GDP between 1988 and 1998. For high income countries the corresponding data are 9.9% and 22.3%, and for the EU, 9.4% and 32.2%. (World Bank, 2000 World Development Indicators). Calculated on the same basis, FDI flows are smaller but also show exponential growth. Again, over the 1988 1998 period, gross FDI rose from 1.7% to 3.8% of world GDP, in high income countries the corresponding data are 2.6% and 5.7%, with more rapid growth in the EU, from 2.1% to 6.1%.

Foreign direct investment

FDI is the driving force of globalisation. It is the practice of firms investing in production facilities in other countries instead of producing goods at home and then exporting them. Thus to an increasing extent, merchandise trade flows are being substituted for by FDI. This form of investment is particularly visible because it often involves very large companies investing in new factories in other countries. In the UK, the obvious example is the investment by Japanese car firms, in UK-based production facilities. Where previously, Japanese cars were imported into the UK in large numbers, now few are imported, most are made in the UK. These conspicuous developments are counterbalanced by the less well known investments of UK companies overseas. Even in the late 1980s the value of outputs produced by UK companies overseas is estimated to have exceeded the total value of UK exports. The same is true of the USA, but not so far of other major economies. The size and growth of FDI in the EU, USA and Japan, are shown in Table 12. The EU's outward flow of FDI in 1997 was equal to 13% of the value of goods exported. At the end of 1996, the EU had FDI assets of 543 billion ECU in other countries, and these exceeded the value of FDI by other countries in the EU by 121 billion ECU. The main recipients of the EU's FDI were USA (43%), Switzerland (9%) and Australia (5%). The EU had FDI net asset positions with nearly all countries and markets.

Why is this movement of firms instead of goods taking place? Consider a car firm. Developing new models requires huge investments

Table 12 Foreign direct investment flows selected years 1991-97 (billion Ecu)

		1991	1994	1997
EU	Outward flows	26.7	24.1	96.4
	Inward flows	20.9	21.8	44.0
USA	Outward flows	12.9	32.9	-
	Inward flows	35.4	36.3	-
Japan	Outward flows	24.8	15.1	22.9
	Inward flows	1.1	0.7	2.8
Intra-EU	flows	37.5	50.3	85.3

Source: *Europe in Figures 2000,* Eurostat.

in design. The greater the number of cars produced, the lower is the average fixed cost of the design. It may be cheaper to use the design in a new factory overseas than it is to export completed cars there. The need to spread fixed costs over larger outputs, and the fact that it may be cheaper to transport technology than the somewhat more bulky products, is the rationale for FDI.

Consequences of FDI

Clearly, the introduction of foreign firms into a domestic market must increase competition. This may be nice for consumers, but what about the domestic producers? Competing producers of the same final product may be forced out of production. On the other hand, suppliers of inputs may benefit. Governments often encourage investments by overseas firms by offering subsidies for them to develop factories, particularly in areas of high unemployment. Are there any motives apart from hopes of increased local employment? One reason for encouraging FDI is that it improves the skills of the workers it employs, which through labour turnover, may be passed on to other businesses. Similarly, supplying firms may be helped directly to produce higher quality intermediate goods, and indirectly through learning improved management practices. In short, government subsidies are provided in the expectation that the **social rate of return** may exceed the **private rate of return** by more than the cost of the subsidy. These hopes for FDI apply both in poor countries, such as the transition economies discussed in Chapter 8, and in rich countries, most of which have regions of relative poverty, or industries which could benefit from technology developed elsewhere.

Evidently both firms and governments consider FDI to be beneficial or the former would not undertake them and the latter would not encourage, or at least tolerate them. Consumers are likely to benefit, but what about labour and employment? Here, the effects depend largely upon the nature of labour markets. In the USA, the lack of social security provisions helps to make the labour market very flexible. So competition in the labour market results in job insecurity and low labour costs and incomes. This has permitted a substantial increase in employment, and in 2000, an unemployment rate of 4.4% In contrast, Europe's social provision for the unemployed is relatively generous, and labour markets are characterised by rigidity. In consequence, in the face of increased competition, labour's wages and incomes have remained stable, but unemployment is substantial. Indeed, unemployment has been identified by the Commission as the EU's major problem. Unemployment of the under 25 age group is particularly high, being approximately double that of the over 25s. During the 1991-95 period unemployment averaged 10%, but then began to fall and in 2000 is forecast to be 8.6%, an improvement but still almost double that of the USA.

Conclusion

Trade has increased substantially in response to the reduction of international trade barriers. Globalisation, the emergence of 'one world', where goods, capital and services flow freely between countries, thanks to the virtual elimination of regulation, is increasing wealth globally. In Europe, the adjustment to increased competition caused by globalisation has been a reduction in employment due to rigidities in the labour market. The challenge to the EU is to improve labour skills, and to take other measures to improve labour mobility.

KEY WORDS

Comparative advantage	World Trade Organisation
Globalisation	(WTO)
General Agreement on Tariffs	Foreign direct investment (FDI)
and Trade (GATT)	Social rate of return
Most favoured nation	Private rate of return
Uruguay Round	

Further reading

Bamford, C. and Grant, S. Chapters 5 and 8 in *The UK Economy in a Global Context*. Heinemann Educational, 2000.

Grant, S. and Vidler, C. Part 2, Unit 12 in *Economics in Context*. Heinemann Educational, 2000.

Sloman, J. Chapter 25 in *Economics*. (4th edn). Pearson Education, 2000.

Useful website

United Nations Economic Commission for Europe: www.unece.org

Essay topics

1. (a) Discuss the sources of conflict between the European Union and other trading blocs.   [40 marks]
   (b) Examine the economic effects of abandoning tariff barriers in the world economy.   [60 marks]

[Edexcel, Unit Test 6 Specimen Paper, Q2, 2000.]
2. (a) Analyse the theoretical benefits and drawbacks of a customs union. [12 marks]
   (b) In the light of these, assess the EU's external trade policy with other developed and developing economies. [8 marks]
[UCLES, Economics of Europe paper, Q3, March 1996.]

Data response question

A likely effect of the creation of the EMU market will in time be a substantial relocation of European business, as companies take advantage of increasing returns by focusing production in one area from which to serve the entire EMU market and to form clusters of activity with similar companies. Businesses from the same sector benefit from locating together for three principal reasons: skilled labour market pooling, the development of specialised local suppliers and technological spillovers from one firm to others. Reduced transactions costs for trade across national borders within the EMU area will encourage the development of business clusters in Europe. Evidence shows that European business sectors are much less clustered in specific areas than their US counterparts. Over time this is likely to change. Furthermore, increasing returns to clustering imply that whichever region gains an initial cost advantage through this process tends to sustain and grow that advantage – accidents of history determine future industrial structure. As long as we remain an 'out', UK business will be on the sidelines of this process, and could become disadvantaged in Europe if businesses within EMU reap benefits from the change. If EMU makes a successful start, by no means guaranteed, this may be the issue that forces an eventual decision to enter.

Source: extract from 'EMU to make uncertain start' by Patrick Foley, *Economic Bulletin*, Lloyds TSB Bank, February 1998.

(a) Explain what is meant by business clusters. [2 marks]
(b) Describe the reasons why business clusters tend to develop. [3 marks]
(c) Discuss the advantages of inward foreign direct investment for a country or region. [6 marks]
(d) Assess whether EMU has made 'a successful start'. [9 marks]

Chapter Eight
Transition economies

...[They] have nothing to lose but their chains. They have a world to win...men of all countries unite. Karl Marx, *The Communist Manifesto* (1848)

Collapse of communism

In 1989 the communist system of east Europe collapsed, to be followed by the break up of the Soviet Union in 1991. Some countries – those dominated by Russian culture – immediately re-grouped as the **Commonwealth of Independent States** (CIS), whilst others, the Baltic States and the **Central and East European Countries** (CEECs), decided to maintain their independence, though most of the latter group decided that their best long-term objective was to join the European Community. See Table 13 for a list of the countries involved (there are 12 CIS countries, the table excludes five which are in Asia).

These groups had one feature in common, the need to change from a communist centrally planned system to a market system under democratic government. Clearly the change from self-perpetuating totalitarian government to governments elected through the free democratic process is fundamental. The concomitant change to free markets is equally so. This is most obvious if the different roles of prices in the two economic systems are compared. Under central planning, prices are merely units of account, production and resource-use being determined by bureaucratic decision, and consumers buy what is available. Free markets work the other way round starting from the consumer, whose purchases guide production and thus the use of resources. The transition from communism to democracy and from planned to free markets results in these countries being dubbed the **transition economies**.

What does transition involve?

Governments, managements, legal institutions, and public administrations were all required to adjust to free markets. The latter includes not only markets for goods, but also for labour, capital and services. Communism had lasted too long for people to have any experience of such things, and huge changes were required, not least in the state industries, which had been monopoly producers and distributors.

Table 13 The transition economies – real GDP, annual percentage changes 1990–99

	1990	1991	1992	1993	1994	1995	1996	1997	1998	1999
CEECs										
Albania	-10.0	-28.0	-7.2	9.6	8.3	13.3	9.1	-7.0	8.0	8.0
Bosnia Hercegovina	-23.2	-12.1	-12.1	-12.1	-12.1	33.0	28.0	0.0	-	-
Bulgaria	-9.1	-11.8	-7.3	-1.5	1.8	2.9	-10.1	-7.0	3.5	2.6
Croatia	-7.1	-21.1	-11.7	-8.0	5.9	6.8	5.0	6.8	2.5	-0.3
Czech Republic	-1.2	-11.5	-3.3	0.6	2.7	6.4	3.9	-1.0	-2.2	-0.2
Hungary	-3.5	-11.9	-3.1	-0.6	2.9	1.5	1.3	4.6	4.9	4.5
Poland	-11.6	-7.0	2.6	3.8	5.2	7.0	6.1	6.9	4.8	4.1
Romania	-5.6	-12.9	-8.8	1.5	3.9	7.1	3.9	-6.1	-5.4	-3.2
Slovakia	-2.5	-14.6	-6.4	-3.7	4.9	6.9	6.6	6.5	4.4	1.9
Slovenia	-8.1	-8.9	-5.5	2.8	5.3	4.1	3.1	4.6	3.9	4.9
FYR Macedonia	-10.2	-7.0	-8.0	-9.1	-1.8	-1.2	0.7	1.4	2.9	2.7
Yugoslavia	-7.9	-11.6	-27.9	-30.8	2.5	6.1	5.9	7.4	2.5	-19.3
Baltic States										
Estonia	-8.1	-10.0	-14.1	-8.5	-1.8	4.3	4.0	10.6	4.0	-1.4
Latvia	2.7	-10.4	-34.9	-14.9	0.6	-0.8	3.3	8.6	3.9	0.1
Lithuania	-3.3	-5.7	-21.3	-14.2	-9.8	3.3	4.7	7.3	5.1	-3.0
CIS										
Armenia	-5.5	-11.7	-41.8	-8.8	5.4	6.9	5.8	3.3	7.2	3.0
Azerbaijan	-11.7	-0.7	-22.6	-23.1	-19.7	-11.8	1.3	5.8	10.0	7.4
Belarus	-2.0	-1.3	-9.5	-7.6	-12.5	-10.4	2.8	11.4	8.4	3.4
Georgia	-15.1	-21.1	-44.9	-29.3	-10.4	2.6	8.6	11.3	2.9	3.0
Republic of Moldova	-1.4	-17.5	-29.0	-1.2	-30.9	-1.9	-7.8	1.6	-8.6	-4.4
Russia	-3.0	-5.0	-14.5	-8.7	-12.7	-4.1	-3.5	0.9	-4.9	3.2
Ukraine	-3.6	-8.7	-9.9	-14.2	-22.9	-12.2	-10.0	-3.0	-1.7	-0.4

Source: United Nations Economic Commission for Europe, *Statistical Yearbook*, various years.

The progress of transition

The communist state-owned industries were typically over-manned and used old technology. The 1989 revolutions were followed by a 'transitional recession' in which both output and employment fell far below their pre-reform levels. In practice output fell much more than employment, governments deeming it wise to keep employment artificially high in the absence of any social security safety net. Thus many virtually unemployed people received miserably low wages so they could continue to receive these and the non-wage benefits of their

Table 14 Unemployment in the transition economies, per cent of total employment 1991-99

	1991	1992	1993	1994	1995	1996	1997	1998	1999
CEECs									
Albania	9.1	24.2	19.5	19.6	13.0	12.0	14.9	17.6	-
Bosnia Hercegovina	-	55.6	77.3	81.5	72.6	72.5	39.0	38.5	39.1
Bulgaria	11.1	15.3	16.4	12.4	11.1	12.5	13.7	12.2	16.0
Croatia	14.9	17.2	16.8	16.7	16.8	10.0	17.6	18.6	20.8
Czech Republic	-	-	3.8	3.9	3.5	4.0	5.2	7.5	9.4
Hungary	-	9.8	11.9	10.7	10.2	9.9	10.4	9.1	9.6
Poland	-	-	14.0	14.4	13.3	12.4	10.3	10.4	13.0
Romania	-	-	-	8.2	8.0	6.7	8.8	10.3	11.5
Slovakia	-	-	-	13.7	13.1	11.1	12.5	15.6	19.2
Slovenia	-	9.1	9.0	7.4	7.3	-	14.8	14.6	13.0
FYR Macedonia	24.5	26.3	27.7	30.0	35.6	36.6	41.7	41.4	47.0
Yugoslavia	-	24.6	24.0	23.9	24.7	26.1	25.6	27.2	27.4
Baltic States									
Estonia	1.8	4.5	7.6	8.9	9.7	10.0	4.6	5.1	6.7
Latvia	-	-	-	-	18.9	18.3	6.7	9.2	9.1
Lithuania	0.3	1.3	4.4	3.6	6.1	7.1	6.7	6.9	10.0
CIS									
Armenia	-	3.5	6.3	6.0	8.1	9.7	11.0	8.9	11.5
Azerbaijan	-	0.2	0.7	0.9	1.1	1.1	1.3	1.4	1.2
Belarus	0.1	0.5	1.3	2.1	2.7	4.0	2.8	2.3	2.0
Georgia	-	0.3	2.0	3.8	3.4	3.2	8.0	4.2	5.6
Republic of Moldova	-	0.7	0.7	1.0	1.4	1.5	1.7	1.9	2.1
Russia	-	4.7	5.5	7.5	8.9	9.3	11.2	13.3	12.3
Ukraine	0.3	0.4	0.3	0.6	1.5	2.8	2.8	2.9	3.1

Source: United Nations Economic Commission for Europe *Statistical Yearbook*, various years. Only the European CIS countries have been included. http://www.unece.org/stats

enterprises as a substitute for social provision. Over-manning also helped to make some other aspects of reform more acceptable, notably the price liberalisation which resulted in soaring inflation, wiping out many peoples' savings and reducing real wages.

These changes were most marked in the CIS countries, where unemployment is seen in Table 14 to remain relatively low, whilst GDP fell dramatically as shown in Table 13. This concealed unemployment delayed the adjustments in labour productivity, which were essential to the reallocation of both labour and other resources. Thus

Figure 5 The present and possible future of the European Union

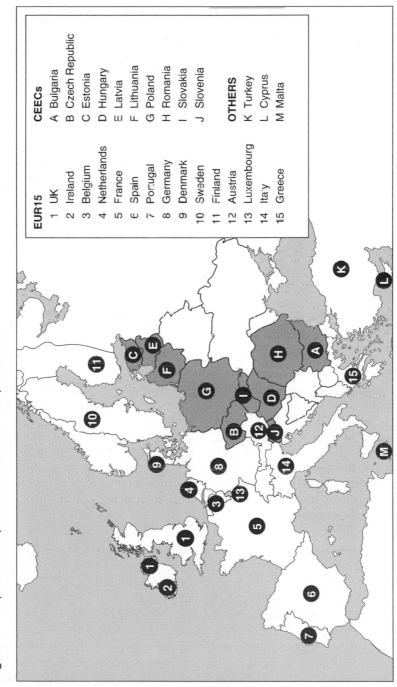

EUR15		CEECs	
1	UK	A	Bulgaria
2	Ireland	B	Czech Republic
3	Belgium	C	Estonia
4	Netherlands	D	Hungary
5	France	E	Latvia
6	Spain	F	Lithuania
7	Portugal	G	Poland
8	Germany	H	Romania
9	Denmark	I	Slovakia
10	Sweden	J	Slovenia
11	Finland		
12	Austria	**OTHERS**	
13	Luxembourg	K	Turkey
14	Italy	L	Cyprus
15	Greece	M	Malta

in Russia, by 1996, GDP was still only 61% of its 1991 level with low levels also being recorded for industrial output (51%) and agricultural output (65%). Over the same period consumer prices increased by a factor of almost 22, a modest increase compared to those of most other CIS countries, the worst being the Ukraine, where prices increased by more than 400 times. As the Tables 13 and 14 show, the CEEC states tended to permit more rapid adjustments, with unemployment rising far more rapidly.

In free markets, one would expect competition to force a shake-out of under-employed labour, with a consequent improvement in labour productivity and a parallel rise in unemployment. Delaying these changes in the CIS countries resulted in their GDPs not beginning to recover until 1996, two years after recovery began in most of the CEECs.

Transition involves both institutional and economic change. Important are macro-economic stability, the rate and success of privatisation, and the introduction of **foreign direct investment** (FDI). The success of privatisation of state industries has been very variable. In some countries, old managers of state industries have not been replaced, greatly slowing the pace of change. Privatisation from bottom up – the introduction of new firms by entrepreneurs – should be successful more rapidly. In this context, it must be noted that '**small and medium sized enterprises**' (SMEs, defined as firms employing up to 100 workers) account for more than half of the total labour force in free market industrialised societies like the EU. The countries where productivity has increased most quickly (e.g. Hungary) by 2000, already had over 20% of employment in SMEs, but these accounted for little employment in most countries. FDI, either through the introduction of new firms, or joint ventures between existing firms and incoming multinationals, should also be important. FDI may have major impacts through the introduction of new technology, modern managerial systems and exposure to competition. In practice FDI has been fairly small so far, but along with the development of SMEs should help to revolutionise management and productivity.

Aid to the CIS

During 1990 the European Council decided to introduce a programme of '**technical assistance to the CIS**' (TACIS). The measures were aimed to help with the transition to market economies and to reinforce democracy. The programme finances grants for the provision of policy advice, consultancy teams, technical training, the development of legal and regulatory frameworks and institutions, the reorganisation of industries, the conversion of defence-related industries and the development of SMEs. By helping with feasibility studies Tacis also helps with access to funding by major lenders. Since its inception Tacis has committed 3.3 billion ECU to over 3000 projects and is formulating a new programme for the period 2000-06.

One of the major areas of assistance has been to the nuclear industry. The Chernobyl nuclear accident of 1986 drew attention to the safety problems of the Soviet-designed nuclear reactors which are found right across east Europe in both CIS and CEEC countries. The EU is working with the International Atomic Energy Authority (United Nations), and the OECD to help the countries of east Europe to make their reactors as safe as those in the west, and helped with the closure of the Chernobyl plant, completed in December 2000.

CEECs

When communism collapsed, Poland, Hungary and Czechoslovakia met at Visegrad (becoming known as the Visegrad countries) to discuss what to do next. They quickly reached the conclusion that they would like to join the European Community, a desire soon expressed by most of the other CEECs. The Community's measures to aid the transition of these countries and to prepare them for eventual membership are detailed in the following chapter.

A decade of transition

The large decline in employment resulting from the required structural adjustments meant that in 1998, employment was still 14% below 1989 levels, over 80% of this decline being in industry. Over the same years GDP was still depressed by 35%.

The sectoral pattern of employment indicates the changes due to transition. The greatest reductions in employment were in agriculture, industry and construction, whilst the major increase was in services. In agriculture, restructuring and privatisation reduced labour employed dramatically in most countries, though in Armenia, Romania and Ukraine there were large increases – resulting from the reintroduction of small private farms and the return of some unemployed labour to its rural roots. In industry the continuous reduction in overemployment caused a decline in its labour force which was still progressing in 1999. A similar situation in construction has probably been exacerbated by a fall in house building and infrastructure construction by the public sector due to budget constraints.

Manufacturing has tended to be the engine of growth in most countries and here, labour has declined less, and has even increased in

Hungary and Poland. Services showed the smallest initial declines in employment because they include the relatively stable health, education and social services. Under central planning, many other services did not exist, and the development of financial services, renting, real estate, wholesale, retail, and repair services in the private sector, along with an expansion of public administration, and increases in hotels and restaurants, have absorbed much of the labour released from elsewhere. Indeed the service sector now accounts for more than 50% of total employment in all countries except Poland.

Conclusions

The transition from central planning to free markets is initially very disruptive, typically year by year reducing both output and employment substantially. Restructuring and recovery is very slow, but does occur. Even after a decade, GDPs remain lower than at the beginning. However, towards the end of the decade the pace of change began to accelerate, although characterised by volatility. The Asian financial crisis and the collapse of the Russian rouble caused significant recessionary pressures in 1998 and the first half of 1999. Yet the transition economies achieved an average growth rate of 2.25% in 1999, the highest figure of the decade. GDP in the CIS countries increased by 2.9%. Russia grew by 3.2%, the highest rate it has experienced since the capitalist revolution, and this was accompanied by its first increase in employment. The countries of south-east Europe were depressed by military conflicts, but in the central European countries the growth rate in both 1998 and 1999 was about 3.2%. In general it appears that the worst of the structural changes have been suffered and these economies are at last emerging from their traumatic pasts.

KEY WORDS

Commonwealth of Newly Independent States (i.e. ex-USSR) (CIS)
(Ex-communist) Central and East European Countries (CEECs)

Transition economies
Foreign direct investment (FDI)
Small and medium sized enterprises (SMEs)
Tacis

Further reading

Bamford, C., (ed.). Chapter 13 in *Economics for AS*. CUP, 2000.

Grant, S. Chapter 4 in *Stanlake's Introductory Economics* (7th edn). Longman, 2000.

Grant, S. and Vidler, C. Part 2, Unit 25 in *Economics in Context*. Heinemann Educational, 2000.

Useful website

Organisation for Economic Co-operation and Development: www.oecd.org/

Essay topics

1. (a) Explain, using economic analysis, why countries in Eastern Europe have made the transition to a market economy.
    [8 marks]

    (b) Discuss why some Eastern European countries have made this transition more successfully and less painfully than others.
    [12 marks]

    [UCLES, Economics of Europe paper, Q3, March 1998.]

2. In the first three years following the collapse of Comecon, the former command economies increased their trade with the European Union (EU) by between 50% and 150%.

    (a) With reference to the case of former command economies, briefly explain:
    (i) the reasons for the growth in trade with the EU;
    (ii) the need for trade liberalisation.   [10 marks]

    (b) Discuss the advantages for these economies of joining the EU.
    [10 marks]

    [OCR, Economics of Europe paper, Q2, March 2000.]

Data response question

Section A

Answer this question on Hungary 'forging closer links with the European Union (EU)'

Hungary was the first of the former Eastern bloc economies to open its doors to free trade and today is the only one which has completely liberalized its import trade. This commitment to free trade is one of the credentials which will stand it in good stead to gain EU membership. Table 1 overleaf shows certain aspects of Hungary's trade from 1991 to 1994.

Table 1 Basic statistics of Hungarian–EU trade, 1991–94

Total trade	1991	1992	1993	1994
Hungarian exports (Ft billion current prices)	764	844	820	772
Hungarian imports (Ft current prices)	844	879	1163	1157
Export to import ratio (%)	91	96	71	67
Trade with the EU				
Hungarian exports (FT billion current prices)	350	419	381	359
Hungarian imports (Ft billion current prices)	352	375	466	462
Export to import ratio (%)	99	112	82	78
Other information				
Exchange rate v. US $ (Index Jan. 1993 = 100)	93	95	100.7	113
External debt (US billion)	na	na	24.6	28.5
Debt ratio (years) *	na	na	1.6	2.0
% Change in consumer prices	18	20	23	19

Ft, Forint, the Hungarian unit of currency.
*Number of years of hard currency income required to repay debt.

(a)　(i)　Why are imports measured at 'current prices'?　　　　[1 mark]
　　　(ii) Explain an alternative way by which the value of imports might be measured.　　　　[2 marks]
(b)　(i)　From Table 1, compare the export to import ratio of total trade with the export to import ratio of Hungary's trade with the EU.　　　　[2 marks]
　　　(ii) Explain the implications of any differences you have observed.　　　　[2 marks]
(c)　(i)　In the period shown, was the Hungarian currency appreciating or depreciating with respect to the US$? Explain your answer.　　　　[2 marks]
　　　(ii) What might be the economic implications of this for the Hungarian economy?　　　　[2 marks]
(d)　Suppose you are a UK consumer goods manufacturer seeking to set up a production plant in Hungary. Explain how the data in Table 1 might be useful to you.　　　　[4 marks]
(e)　Comment upon the economic implications of the debt problems facing the Hungarian economy.　　　　[5 marks]
[UCLES, Economics of Europe paper, Q1, June 1997.]

Chapter Nine
Further enlargements to the south and east

'... any European State may apply to become a member ...' Article
237 of the Treaty of Rome

In the previous chapter it was noted that some of the CEECs wished to
join the EU. Ten have applied for membership. To the south, Turkey,
Cyprus and Malta also wish to join. Table 15 gives some basic information about the applicant countries and the EU. It shows that if all
thirteen countries joined simultaneously, they would have 37% of the
land area, 31% of the population, but only a little over 6% of the GDP
of an EU28. Clearly, this huge disparity in income would be a major
problem. For most of these countries there is also some transitional
change to be completed. The EU would also face difficulties unless its
current institutional structure and economic policies are reformed. In
this chapter we consider the problems and policies relating to these
proposed further enlargements, first in preparing the applicants countries for accession, second in preparing the EU for their acceptance.

Europe Agreements
These are the basic legal instruments defining relations between the
applicant countries and the Community. Beginning in 1991 they gradually replaced the original trade and cooperation arrangements and by
1996 each of the ten CEECs noted in the Table 15 had signed these
new association agreements. Their long-term function is gradually to
align the CEECs' economic and legal systems with those of the EU in
preparation for ultimate membership.

At the Copenhagen Council, in 1993, the Heads of State and
Government confirmed that applicant CEECs could join *as soon as
they fulfilled the economic and political requirements* for membership.
This Council specified the criteria which had to be satisfied before an
applicant could join. The 'Copenhagen Criteria' which must be
achieved by an applicant country are:

• stability of institutions guaranteeing democracy, the rule of law,
  human rights and protection of minorities
• the existence of a functioning market economy as well as the capacity to cope with competitive pressure and market forces within the
  Union

Table 15 Applicant countries – area, population and relative incomes, 1998

	Area 1000 km²	Population 1000s	GDP bn ECU	Per capita GDP % EU15 average
Bulgaria	111	8230	11.0	23
Cyprus*	9.2	663	8.1	78
Czech Republic	79	10290	50.1	60
Estonia	45	1446	4.6	36
Hungary	93	10092	42.4	49
Latvia	65	2439	5.7	27
Lithuania	65	3701	9.5	31
Malta	0.3	378	3.1	-
Poland	313	38667	140.7	39
Romania	238	22489	33.9	27
Slovakia	49	5393	18.1	46
Slovenia	20	1978	17.4	68
Turkey	775	63451	175.8	37
Applicants totals	1862.5	169217	520.4	38
EU15	3191	374888	7585.6	100

*Cyprus: area is the whole island, population and GDP figures relate to the government controlled part only.
Source: EU Press Release, 7.12.99.

- the ability to take on the obligations of membership including adherence to the political, economic and monetary union
- the conditions for its integration so that European Community legislation can be transposed into national legislation and implemented effectively through appropriate administrative and judicial structures.

A 'twinning' programme has been introduced to help the applicant countries to develop their administrations and institutions in preparation for the application of Community legislation. Twinning means the secondment of advisers from the EU Member States' own administrations to work alongside their counterparts in the CEECs.

PHARE programme

This is the financial instrument supporting the achievement of the objectives of the Europe Agreements. PHARE was initially set up in 1989 to help with the massive economic restructuring and political change required following the collapse of communism. **PHARE** (Pologne, Hungrie, assistance pour la restructuration économique) at first applied only to Poland and Hungry but was later extended to the other CEECs. Between 1989 and 1999 the Community committed Ecu 11 billion to this programme.

After the Copenhagen Council invited the CEECs to apply formally for membership, Phare became the means of guiding the applicant countries' transitions to prepare them for accession. In 1997 the fund became focused entirely on the pre-accession priorities identified in each country. Two new financial mechanisms were introduced in 1999, a pre-accession structural instrument (**ISPA**) to improve transport and environmental protection infrastructures, and a pre-accession agricultural instrument (**SAPARD**) designed to encourage the long-term adjustment of agriculture and rural areas. Phare 2000-06 is providing a further Ecu 11 billions to help the applicant CEECs to prepare for accession.

Accession negotiations

In 1998 accession negotiations began with Hungary, Poland, Estonia, the Czech Republic, Slovenia and Cyprus. Negotiations with Bulgaria, Latvia, Lithuania, Malta, Romania and Slovakia opened in 2000. The Commission has proposed an accession partnership with Turkey, but actual accession negotiations with this country will be delayed because it fails to fulfil the political criteria – the EU considering that Turkey

Table 16 Phare, annual allocations for restructuring in the CEEC applicant countries 2000-06 (Ecu millions)

	PHARE	SAPARD	ISPA	TOTAL
Bulgaria	100	52.1	83.2	124.8
Czech Republic	79	22.1	57.2	83.2
Estonia	24	12.1	20.8	36.4
Hungary	96	38.1	72.8	104
Latvia	30	21.8	36.4	57.2
Lithuania	42	29.8	41.6	62.4
Poland	398	168.7	312	384.8
Romania	242	150.6	208	270.4
Slovakia	49	18.3	36.4	57.2
Slovenia	25	6.3	10.4	20.8
Total	1577	520	1040	2645

Source: Press release 27/10/00.

should decide to translate its intentions concerning human rights into actions.

In November 2000 the Commission reported on the situation in each applicant country with respect to both the political and economic criteria. On the political side, it notes improvements in the quality of democratic institutions, in the rule of law and the protection of human rights, but calls for further reforms of the judiciary, and is concerned at the prevalence of corruption. The economic criteria refer to the functioning of the market system and the ability to cope with competitive forces. It believes that Cyprus and Malta already meet the economic criteria, and that Estonia, Hungary and Poland should meet these criteria in the 'near term' if they continue with their current reforms. Similar 'near term' status is accorded to the Czech Republic and Slovenia if they implement some remaining reforms. Latvia, Lithuania and Slovakia should meet the criteria in the 'medium term', whilst Bulgaria, Romania and Turkey still have to make much more progress.

No specific time periods are attached to these 'near' and 'medium term' expressions. Indeed, the accession of any country will take place when it meets all the political and economic criteria, and the implied order of accession listed above may not apply in practice. However the EU is committed to complete its own internal reforms, essential before further enlargement, by the end of 2002, and the Commission expects that some countries will accede perhaps as early as 2003, but certainly within the lifetime of the current Commission, which ends on 22 January 2005.

When a country does join the EU it is unlikely to be devoid of problems, and some transitional arrangements will be necessary. The acceding countries may request such arrangements to enable them to complete minor aspects of their convergence. The EU may also wish to have transitional arrangements to reduce impacts on its common policies, such as those relating to consumers, health, the environment or the budget.

Preparing the EU for enlargement

In Chapter 1 it was noted that under the Treaty of Rome decisions were to be reached unanimously in the early years, but that later, decisions were to be reached through **qualified majority voting** (QMV). In the event, member states were reluctant to drop their powers of veto, and as more countries joined, reaching decisions became increasingly difficult. Indeed, the Community seemed to be grinding to a halt, until it was 'relaunched' by the Single European Act, which *inter alia*, introduced qualified majority voting for most commercial decisions. Still many areas were left subject to veto powers, and getting unanimity in a Community of 15 proved to be difficult, making action on some topics very slow. Clearly in a substantially enlarged EU, unanimity will be extremely difficult, and the need for QMV becomes more pressing. Similarly, the Commission, Parliament and other institutions would also become unduly cumbersome if enlargement resulted in their proportional expansions. Preparing EU decision making and institutions for enlargement was the business of the Inter-Governmental Council (IGC), which began meetings at ministerial level in February 2000, and completed its deliberations at Heads of Government level in Nice in December 2000. The main issues relevant to enlargement which were decided at Nice are:

- the size and composition of the European Commission
- the weighting of votes in the Council
- the extension of qualified majority voting in the Council
- the allocation of seats in the European Parliament.

The Commission has always been comprised of two Commissioners from each of the larger member countries and one each from the smaller members. The original Commission had nine Commissioners, and expanded with each enlargement until it reached 20 Commissioners in 1995 with the last enlargement. Continuing with such expansions would have resulted in 35 Commissioners by the time the currently negotiating twelve extra members had acceded. Decisions taken at Nice will allow the Commission to grow to 26 with the accession of the first six new EU members. Then it will be subject to a major reorganisation to keep numbers down, notably with the five largest member states each being restricted to one, instead of the current two Commissioners. Some of the smaller states may have to have Commissioners on a rotational basis. One major change is that the President will be elected by a majority vote of member states instead of the current requirement of unanimity. In a further change, the President will have the power to dismiss Commissioners, wide discretion in the assignment of portfolios, and in the appointment of Vice-Presidents.

Over 90% of Council decisions are reached by QMV. The numbers of votes given to member states are not in exact proportion to the sizes of their populations, because this would allow the larger countries to impose their wishes upon the smaller countries (see Chapter 1). The current allocation of votes and the changes agreed at Nice are shown in Table 17. It will be seen that under the new allocation of votes the

Table 17 Changes in the allocation of Council votes and Parliamentary seats from 1st January 2005

	Population million	Current votes	New votes	Parliamentary seats allocation	
				Old	New
Germany	82.0	10	29	99	99
UK	59.2	10	29	87	72
France	59.0	10	29	87	72
Italy	57.6	10	29	87	72
Spain	39.4	8	27	64	50
Netherlands	15.8	5	13	31	25
Greece	10.5	5	12	25	22
Belgium	10.2	5	12	25	22
Portugal	10.0	5	12	25	22
Sweden	8.8	4	10	22	18
Austria	8.1	4	10	21	17
Denmark	5.3	3	7	16	13
Finland	5.2	3	7	16	13
Ireland	3.7	3	7	15	12
Luxembourg	0.4	2	4	6	6
Candidate countries					
Poland	38.7	-	27	-	50
Romania	22.5	-	14	-	33
Czech Republic	10.3	-	12	-	20
Hungary	10.1	-	12	-	20
Bulgaria	8.2	-	10	-	17
Slovakia	5.4	-	7	-	13
Lithuania	3.7	-	7	-	12
Latvia	2.4	-	4		8
Slovenia	2.0	-	4	-	7
Estonia	1.4	-	4	-	6
Cyprus	0.8	-	4	-	6
Malta	0.4	-	3	-	5

Source: Draft Treaty of Nice, http://ue.eu.int/cigdocs/en/cig2000-EN

proportional share of votes has been moved in favour of the larger states. This is to prevent the possibility of the larger states – who have the bulk of the EU population – being dominated by the large number of smaller states in an enlarged Community. In 2005, if the EU still has 15 members, its QMV in Council would be as shown in Table 17, and a qualified majority would be 170 cast by at least a majority of the members – if the proposal being voted on originated with the Commission. In other cases the majority is still 170 but it must be cast by at least two thirds of the members. In addition, any member may request verification that the qualified majority comprises at least 62% of the total population of the Union. In an EU of 27 with a total of 345 votes, 258 votes would be a qualified majority, but in addition to the implied blocking minority of 88 there are two other ways of forming a blocking minority. First, a majority of countries against a proposal can block it – as a protection for the smaller countries. Second, the 62% of EU population test noted above can be applied. These somewhat byzantine additions to QMV will not make decisions easier to reach.

QMV already applies to most Council decisions, but with significant topics still subject to national vetoes – before Nice there were 70 in all. The Commission had hoped for most of the latter to disappear at this conference, but only 29 were removed. Spain insisted on its veto in respect of cohesion funds after 2006, clearly expecting thus to ensure further major benefits from them. France maintained its veto on trade which might affect French culture, such as audio-visual services and education. Denmark and Greece kept their vetoes on maritime transport, Germany blocked QMV on the free movement of professionals, and the UK kept its vetoes on taxation and social security. So progress towards more QMV was made, but numerous important areas subject to unanimity remain.

The number of Members of the European Parliament is currently 626, and any major increase would make Parliament unwieldy. The **Treaty of Amsterdam** in 1997 limited the future size of Parliament to 700, but at Nice an increase to 728 was agreed for an EU of 27 states. Table 17 shows how the seats would be allocated.

The **Treaty of Nice** has to be ratified by every member state before it can come into operation. There is much to be done in the immediate future if all of the preparations and negotiations are to allow the first of the new wave of accessions by the envisaged date of 2003.

Conclusion

Further enlargements are imminent. The effects on the EU as well as the new members will be substantial, and in the long term should bring greater prosperity to all. At least as important will be the effective protection and expansion of democracy. In all these changes the EU has expressed its wish to aid some of its other poorer European neighbours – both the recently warring Balkan States, and the CIS countries. Although the Balkans could feature in a future enlargement, the CIS countries are not regarded as potential EU members.

```
┌─────────────────────────────────────────────────────────┐
│                      KEY WORDS                          │
│                                                         │
│  Europe agreement          Inter-Governmental Council   │
│  PHARE                       (IGC)                      │
│  Qualified majority voting   Treaty of Amsterdam        │
│    (QMV)                     Treaty of Nice             │
└─────────────────────────────────────────────────────────┘
```

Further reading

Anderton, A. Unit 98 in *Economics* (3rd edn). Causeway Press, 2000.

Grant, S. Chapter 64 in *Stanlake's Introductory Economics* (7th edn). Longman, 2000.

Romer, S. Chapter 8 in *Understanding the European Union*. Anforme, 2000.

Useful website

EU's site on enlargement: www.europa.eu.int/comm/enlargement

Essay topics

1. (a) Explain the reforms which have been necessary in the transition of former command economies in Eastern Europe towards the market system.   [8 marks]
    (b) Discuss the likely economic problems arising from closer integration of Eastern European economies with those of the European Union.   [12 marks]
    [UCLES, Economics of Europe paper, Q3, June 1998.]
2. (a) Explain the objectives of the EU's Common Agricultural Policy (CAP).   [10 marks]
    (b) Comment upon the extent to which there is a misallocation of resources as a consequence of the CAP.   [10 marks]
    [UCLES, Economics of Europe paper, Q2, June 1997.]

Data response question

Prospects of enlargement

The enlarged EU will offer a huge single market to business, with common standards, and without important trade barriers. On the world stage, the union will see its role as a trading superpower enhanced in relations with the other big actors – America, Japan and eventually China. The challenge will be to maintain its decision making capacity despite its size.

Business has moved fastest in accepting the reality of enlargement, investing in the emerging markets of central Europe even before they join the EU. Accession is likely to give new momentum to that process, which has slowed as the negotiations dragged on. The existence of clear competition rules and enforceable commercial law in the courts is certain to give greater confidence to companies that have hitherto looked on the central European markets with caution.

One question-mark stands over when the accession candidates join economic and monetary union, and adopt the euro as their currency. Most are ready to do so as soon as they legally can – within two years of accession. But EU central bankers have misgivings at the idea of expanding the euro-zone so rapidly to include countries whose economies remain fragile.

Another issue is the timetable for freedom of labour movement to be applied between the new members and the old. Germany and Austria are both seeking extended periods of adjustment, in order to protect their own labour markets.

Source: extract from 'Rich man's club prepares to admit new members' by Quentin Peel, *Financial Times*, 19/1/01.

(a) Identify two reasons why a country could seek to join the EU.
[4 marks]
(b) Explain why firms are increasing their investment in the applicant countries. [6 marks]
(c) Assess the risks involved in expanding the euro-zone too rapidly. [6 marks]
(d) Discuss why some current EU members are concerned about the issue of freedom of labour movement between the prospective new members and themselves. [4 marks]

Chapter Ten
Impact of membership on the UK

This royal throne of kings, this scept'red isle
This earth of majesty, this seat of Mars,
This other Eden, demi-paradise, . . .
With inky blots, and rotten parchment bonds;
That England, that was wont to conquer others,
Hath made a shameful conquest of itself.

John of Gaunt, in Shakespeare's *Richard II*

There are still some in the UK who see membership of the European Union as the surrender of **sovereignty** – whether they are right or as out of date as John of Gaunt is a matter of personal opinion. Political opinion in the UK remains split; Labour, Liberal Democrat, and many Conservative Members of Parliament are pro-Europe, but a significant number of right wing Conservatives are very strongly opposed. Prior to the election of Labour in 1997, deep divisions in the Conservative government made the UK very uncooperative and soured UK dealings with the EU. In November 1990 the deputy Prime Minister, Sir Geoffrey Howe, resigned his post on the grounds that he disagreed profoundly with Prime Minister Mrs Thatcher's approach to the EC. This encouraged Mr Heseltine, who had himself resigned from the Cabinet over a European issue some years previously, to challenge Mrs Thatcher for the Conservative party leadership. The subsequent election competition forced Mrs Thatcher to resign, and Mr John Major became the new Prime Minister. These changes in the Conservative leadership failed to heal the divisions, which were soon exposed again in vituperous debates over Maastricht (the Treaty of European Union - TEU). The boxed article opposite is from *The European* of October 1992, giving the views of Baroness Thatcher. At the start of the new millenium Baroness Thatcher's denigration of Europe and demands that it should concentrate on matters such as helping the ex-communist countries seem very out of date, since that is what the EU is doing and intended to do anyway. Although the article is over nine years old it still sums up the right wing case admirably. These views contrast sharply with those of the pro-European wing of the Conservatives. Their views are well expressed by Chris Patten, an ex-Conservative Minister, in the following boxed article.

Whatever his own views, Mr Major was unable to agree to all of

Baroness Thatcher says why she sees the treaty as an outdated vision of Europe

Like many of my fellow Tories, I too have a favourite quotation from Disraeli. At Manchester in 1872 he said that "the programme of the Conservative Party is to maintain the Constitution of the country". This Conservative government, like its predecessors, should have as its main priority the maintenance of our constitutional freedoms, our democratic institutions, and the accountability of Parliament to the people. Because I believe in these principles so deeply I cannot support the ratification of the Maastricht treaty, and I welcome sterling's departure from the Exchange Rate Mechanism (ERM).

The treaty will hand over more powers to unelected bureaucrats, and erode the freedoms of ordinary men and women in this country. And no mere declaration on subsidiarity is going to change the Articles or the thrust of the treaty itself – even assuming that more notice is taken of such a declaration than of those I insisted be appended to the Single European Act.

Our political debate on the Maastricht treaty and the future development of Europe has been conducted in, if possible, even less rational terms than our discussion of exchange rates. We are warned from home and abroad, that it would be a national humiliation if Britain were left in the "slow lane" while others sped towards economic and monetary union. We risk being relegated, it is delicately hinted, to the "second tier" of a two-tier Europe. We must not miss the Continental Express. We must be at the "heart" of Europe. But, as Lord Salisbury once pointed out, half the errors in politics come from taking metaphors literally.

There have been two visions of Europe competing with each other in recent years. There is, first, the federalist vision of a Europe run increasingly from Brussels, united by a common citizenship, harmonised by bureaucratic regulations, equipped with common economic, budgetary, foreign and defence policies, using a single currency and acquiring all the flags, anthems and symbols of nation-hood: all in all, a United States of Europe in embryo.

Then there is what might be called the "confederal" concept of a Europe of national states, based upon the idea of co-operation between independent sovereign countries loosely linked in a free trade area, with competition between different tax and regulatory systems and with freely floating currencies. This "confederal" Europe would accommodate the countries of eastern Europe and give them a reasonable stability. It would maintain, not jeopardise, our relationship with Europe's great friend and protector, the United States.

It is time to get our priorities right. There are more urgent things for Europe to attend to now than Maastricht. It must further free trade by completing the Uruguay round of Gatt. It must strengthen links with America, inside and outside Nato. Above all, it must use both free trade and security to help ex-communist nations build prosperity and entrench freedom.

Britain needs to regain the confidence that we can manage our own affairs successfully once more. And we need a clearly defined economic policy to encourage soundly-based growth. Maastricht can do nothing to assist but much to damage progress towards those objectives. The government must recognise that Maastricht, like the ERM, is part of the vision of yesterday. It is time to set out the vision for tomorrow.

Baroness Thatcher was British Prime Minister from 1979 to 1990.

SOVEREIGNTY AND DEMOCRACY IN
THE EUROPEAN UNION

In the Chatham Lecture at Trinity College, Oxford, Commissioner for External Relations Chris Patten will argue today that too much weight has been placed on sovereignty in the British debate on Europe. The more important concept is that of democracy. He considers why people feel alienated from the EU, and surveys some of the ideas which have been advanced for overcoming the so-called democratic deficit. This is an urgent task, because: 'Only if people accept the legitimacy of the changing political order will they willingly accept the obligations imposed by it. If they do not feel adequately involved and consulted, they will eventually question their political obligation.'

There has been too much focus on sovereignty in the UK debate: 'sovereignty, in the sense of unfettered freedom of action, is a nonsense. A man, naked, hungry and alone in the middle of the Sahara desert is free in the sense that no-one can tell him what to do. He is sovereign, then. But he is also doomed. It is often preferable to accept constraints on freedom of action in order to achieve some other benefit.' As Mrs Thatcher said in 1975: 'Almost every major nation has been obliged by the pressures of the post-war world to pool significant areas of sovereignty so as to create more effective political units.'

By standing back from the EU in the 1950s to preserve its *de jure* sovereignty, Britain reduced its influence over its destiny. Opponents of the EU point to Switzerland or Norway to demonstrate that Britain could be perfectly successful, economically, outside the Union. 'They are not wholly wrong ... I have no doubt we would be less well off outside than in. But there would be no catastrophe; no Biblical plagues. The more important point is that far from gaining sovereignty, in the *de facto* sense, Britain would actually lose it. In international trade we would have to follow WTO rules with little opportunity of shaping them. That would be left to the heavy hitters: the EU and the US. Most of our trade, of course, would still be with countries of the European Union. We would still have to meet Single Market rules (as Switzerland and Norway must). But we would have no say in the shaping of those rules ... Above all, in my view, we would betray our heritage by abandoning the leadership of Europe to a continental combine.'

Much the same, he suggests, could apply to the Euro. 'Britain is no longer part of the inner circle of economic policy-making in the EU - the so-called Eurogroup. Gordon Brown does not always bother to attend the traditional meetings of the 15 Finance Ministers (the ECOFIN Council). That is perhaps understandable insofar as the most enticing smells are starting to emerge from the Eurogroup kitchen - with some of the ECOFIN menu pre-cooked there ... As greater consensus begins to develop in the Eurogroup on economic, monetary and even fiscal issues, I suspect that the economic and competitive pressures upon Britain to come into line, in her own interest, could become very great.'

The more important issue is that of democracy.

At present, people are feeling 'sullen and alienated from the EU not just in Britain, but more widely'. Mr Patten offers various reasons for this. The fundamental one is a lack of democratic underpinning.

How can people be given more say, and feel that they have it? The most obvious remedies (more powers for the European Parliament, an elected Commission) do not meet the case because 'they would further develop the authority of European institutions at the expense of national Parliaments. The EU, as a hybrid between an international institution and a supranational one, is unique. It has made tremendous strides in binding the continent together. But it has to accept that there is no European 'demos' in the sense of a population which feels itself to be one.'

To address the question of democratic accountability, Mr Patten considers:

- including a proportion of delegates from national Parliaments in the European Parliament;
- creating a Second Chamber of the EP;
- holding elections to the EP on the same day as national elections;
- encouraging national Parliaments to engage more wholeheartedly in the European enterprise. (In Britain, for example, MEPs might be members of the Upper House: 'Westminster ... should begin to take responsibility for European outcomes');
- establishing a Foreign Relations Committee of the Union drawing its members from both the EP and national Parliaments;
- defining more clearly where the boundaries lie between national and Community prerogatives;
- making clear within the Treaty that 'ever closer union' does not mean 'ever dwindling nations' and that the long-term destiny of the EU is to work in harmony with its Member States, not to subsume them.

The UN, the IMF, the WTO and other international institutions must also learn how to build democratic legitimacy and emotional commitment. But the issue is especially acute in Europe because the EU is so powerful. It is critical for Europe's future that this problem - 'one of the great puzzles of modern times' - should be solved.

EU Press Notice 26th October 2000

the elements of the TEU because of his right wing's stance. Specifically, he refused UK participation in the social policy (see Chapter 5), and insisted that any final decision on the UK joining a future EMU must be the prerogative of the government of the day. In the event, he was unable to persuade all of his right wing MPs to vote with the government, and ratification of the TEU was only possible because of the support of the Liberal Democrats – Labour voted against on the grounds that the UK should have accepted the whole of the Treaty rather than its mutilated remains (with the Social Chapter missed out, and an EMU opt out put in). The Conservatives in opposition under Mr Hague have moved further to the right, and now attack anything to do with the EU with no attempt at intellectual debate. This political background underlines the depth of controversy which relations between the UK and EU generate. They have been noted here because it is essential for economists to recognize and take account of the political aspects of their analyses, but it must be emphasised that *in their economic analyses economists must remain as far as possible unbiased*. So we now turn from noting political events to asking the factual question – what is the economic impact of EU membership?

It is evident that joining has greatly reduced the policy choices available to the British government. More and more decisions are taken by the Union jointly rather than by Britain independently. Thus if the UK has a balance of payments problem, membership rules out the use of import controls or subsidies to help UK firms. Competition policy is increasingly determined in Brussels. For some years all major policy decisions affecting agriculture have been taken at Union level. *But common action can be very beneficial, the single European market could only be achieved through collective decision-making.*

The economic benefits of membership

Table 18 gives some of the main economic indicators for the UK economy. It shows significant changes in the UK rate of growth since accession to the Community in 1973. In 1974-85 the rate of economic growth was much lower than in the decade before accession. In 1986-90 economic growth resumed at the relatively high rate of 3.3%. In 1990-92 the UK suffered negative growth (a contradiction in terms but conventional usage) so that the average growth rate for 1991-95 was again very low. Since then growth rates have improved and average 2.7 for the period 1996-2000. What factors lay behind these changes in growth rates? The 1974-85 low growth period is not necessarily due to any negative impact of EC membership; it is easily explained by external events. In 1974 the world price of oil increased by almost 400

Table 18 Evolution of the UK economy, 1961–2000

	1961 to 1973	1974 to 1985	1986 to 1990	1991	1996	1997	1998	1999	2000 forecast
GDP annual real growth rate (%)	3.2	1.4	3.3	1.6	2.6	3.5	2.2	1.8	3.4
Gross fixed capital formation (% share of GDP)	20.1	19.2	20.3	18.2	16.9	17.2	17.9	18.6	19.5
Labour productivity growth rate (%)	2.9	1.5	1.5	2.3	1.3	1.7	1.1	0.4	2.0
Employment annual change (%)	0.3	−0.1	1.9	−0.7	1.0	1.8	1.0	1.4	1.4
Unemployment rate (%)	1.9	6.9	9.0	9.5	8.2	7.0	6.3	6.1	5.7
Government debt as % GDP	66.8	54.1	35.0	52.0	52.6	51.0	48.1	45.5	41.6
Inflation rate	5.1	12.4	5.9	3.5	3.3	2.9	3.2	2.2	2.4

Source: *European Economy*, vol. 69, 1999.

per cent, followed by further significant increases at the end of the decade. This was a major factor in precipitating a worldwide depression, *so low growth rates were then the norm in all industrialized countries, although the UK was well below the EC average.* 1979 saw the election of Mrs Thatcher's government and the introduction of radical economic ideas. That administration would undoubtedly claim the credit for the improved growth rate which followed, although growth was only at the EC average. *What is beyond doubt is the fact that the depth of the recession in the early 1990s can be blamed on two UK government mistakes* (in the EU over this period there was a much milder recession). By 1986, a rapidly rising balance of payments deficit demonstrated that demand was growing faster than the ability of UK firms to expand supplies, the gap being filled by imports. Nevertheless further huge increases in demand were to come. In the 1988 budget, large income tax cuts were supposed to lead to expanded output through increased incentives, Chancellor Lawson said in his budget speech

> *'The way to a strong economy is to boost incentives and enterprise. And that means, among other things, keeping income tax as low as possible. Excessive rates of income tax destroy enterprise.'*

There may be some truth in this proposition, but the tax changes expanded aggregate demand far more than they increased aggregate supply, thus raising prices – the rate of inflation – and sucking in even more imports. To combat the surge in inflation *interest rates were progressively raised, from 7.5 per cent in May 1988 to 15 percent in*

October 1989, at which extremely high level they stayed for the next twelve months. In October 1990 the interest rate was reduced by 1 per cent and simultaneously the then Chancellor, *Mr John Major, took sterling into the ERM at too high an exchange rate.* His successor as Chancellor, Mr Norman Lamont, ended up trying to defend an over-valued pound at its ERM-fixed rate. If a rate is to be maintained against the judgements of the markets, it has to be by increasing the rate of interest. So interest rates remained high although the domestic economy desperately needed them to be reduced.

During the boom of 1986-88 firms and businesses had borrowed heavily, house prices had also boomed and many people had taken out large mortgages. Soon all were to find their repayments hugely swollen by the unexpectedly high interest rates. Consumers cut back their expenditures, investment fell, firms and businesses began to go bankrupt with consequent job losses, leading to further falls in demand. As many people lost their firms, businesses, jobs and homes the government maintained high interest rates to hold the exchange rate of sterling in the ERM. Eventually, large-scale speculators realised that the sterling exchange rate could not be held and enor-mous capital flows began. The Prime Minister and the Chancellor of the Exchequer both made public announcements that the rate of exchange would be maintained. The ERM system permits countries in such a situation to agree a devaluation of their currencies, but despite promptings from other EU members the British government stubbornly refused to do this, preferring to pour huge sums into the foreign exchanges. At one time it was spending at the rate of £2 bil-lion per hour, before having to admit ignominious defeat – one speculator, George Soros, made a profit of £650 million. The losses made by the British government, on behalf of taxpayers, exceeded £4 billion. Sterling was forced out of the ERM in September 1992. Subsequent reductions in interest rates were very welcome, but recovery from a recession of the depth which the government caused, was slow.

Table 18 illustrates some of the features of these events. During the first half of the 1990s economic growth was slow, unemployment was high and government debt increased substantially from the low levels achieved by the Thatcher administration. Why was labour productiv-ity growth rate so high compared to its trend value? In a depression, it is the least productive who are the first to become unemployed, thus giving a boost to the growth in labour productivity of *those who are employed.*

The Conservative governments of 1979 to 1996 brought about a change in labour mobility because they favoured unemployment as the way to keep down wages and inflation, and successfully fought union attempts to defend jobs. But keeping unemployment higher than it need be reduces national output and income, and at the same time costs large sums in social payments. Much of the rapid improvement under the Labour government elected in 1997 is due to its ability to reduce unemployment, thus reducing social costs and at the same time increasing GDP. Making the Bank of England entirely independent and handing over the control of the money supply to it, one of the new government's first actions, helped to make clear its commitment to low inflation. A tight fiscal policy and gradual reduction of government debt, in a low inflation environment, have improved business confidence, demonstrated by the gradual increase in fixed capital investment. The influence of labour markets in harnessing the benefits of globalisation are discussed in Chapter 7; it is noticeable that the Labour government is determined to retain a relatively flexible labour market and at the Nice Conference (Chapter 9) maintained its veto over social security matters in Europe.

The account of the UK economy's performance in Table 18 makes it clear that membership of the EU is no panacea; it leaves much scope for national competence or incompetence. But surely other governments are also less than perfect and the UK economy should not be examined in isolation, how does it compare with the EU average? In 1960 the UK enjoyed a substantially higher **GDP per head** (income) than the average of the other members. By the time of accession the UK had lost this advantage. In the 1980s the relative position of the UK improved slightly, and in the late years of the decade GNP per head was 2-3% above the EU average. Alas, the government's economic policies then caused the UK's relative position to plunge by 8% between 1989 and 1991. There has since been some improvement, notably under the Labour government, which came to power in 1997, so by the start of the new millenium the UK's GDP per head was 2% above the EU15 average.

It is impossible to say how much of the credit or blame for the UK's relative economic performance lies with UK governments, and how much affect EU membership has had. However, if trends between 1960 and accession had continued to the present day, the UK's relative GDP would have fallen by now to be little over half that of our EU neighbours. The fact that in 2000 it is slightly more than the EU average supports (but does not prove) the hypothesis that membership has been beneficial – at least it does not appear to have been harmful.

Table 19 GNP per head in the UK compared to EUR15 (*EUR15 = 100*)

1960	121.6
1970	102.8
1980	95.7
1990	99.5
1991	96.3
1992	97.2
1993	98.2
1994	97.7
1995	95.4
1996	98.1
1997	101.5
1998	101.8
1999	102.0
2000	102.7*

*Forecast; comparisons based on purchasing power standard (PPS).

Source: *European Economy 69,* 1999.

The problem of agriculture

Problems arise largely because CAP prices have been supported at levels considerably in excess of those ruling in world markets. It is hoped that the latest reforms of the policy will bring internal prices much nearer to world levels. However, due to the high internal market prices ruling in the past, this much criticised policy has had four major negative influences on the UK.

- Misallocation of resources

Agriculture has been much more heavily protected than the manufacturing sector, so significant **resource misallocation** has occurred. Resources used by agriculture could have been used more productively in other sectors. High food prices push up labour costs and thus reduce international competitiveness. Dumping food surpluses on world markets helps to reduce the costs of some competitors (Japan is a major food importer), and makes other food exporters poorer thus reducing their demand for UK and other EU exports.

- Trade diversion

Before accession the UK purchased food imports at low world market prices. Since accession, much food has been purchased from other member countries at the much higher internal prices.

- **Support costs**

In the first fifteen years of membership the budgetary costs of supporting European agriculture fell disproportionately heavily upon the UK.
Much budgetary expenditure was to pay for the disposal of agricultural surpluses – mainly produced by other members. In the 1970s
only the UK and Germany were net contributors to the budget. The
UK's large net contributions were acknowledged to be unfair and a
correction mechanism was introduced to take account of this. In 1984
this correction was agreed as the repayment of 66% of the difference
between the UK's VAT-related payment and its receipts from the budget. When the GNP-based contributions were introduced (see Chapter
1) this formula was applied to the UK's VAT plus its GNP contributions. As agricultural price support has declined in relative terms, the
budgetary costs of agriculture have declined. At the same time the budget revenues have in the main, become based on ability to pay. So, as
noted in Chapter 1, the EU budget now transfers income from richer
to poorer members, and can no longer be said to be unfair to the UK.
Some aspects of the changing balance of net contributions can be seen
in Table 20.

Whether the benefits and burdens of the EU budget are fairly distributed is difficult to say. The receipts side is distorted because

Table 20 Net contributions to the EU budget, various years (Ecu
millions)

	1980	1988	1994	1995	1996	1997	1998
Belgium	−273	−995	−307	−268	746	−1042	−1428
Denmark	334	351	188	353	193	22	−192
Germany	−1670	−6107	−13834	−10895	−12941	−12224	−10466
Greece		1492	3813	3438	3933	4207	4566
Spain		1334	3006	7440	5972	5936	6483
France	380	−1781	−2801	−1834	−460	−1506	−1718
Ireland	687	1159	1727	1724	2260	2595	2135
Italy	681	124	−2806	−1250	−1402	−1222	−2111
Luxembourg	−5	−67	250	−42	−79	−64	−134
Netherlands	395	1150	−1811	−1794	−2446.8	−2273	−3047
Austria				−1008	−272	−813	−822
Portugal		515	1881	2661	2774	2327	2824
Finland				−219	27	−99	−229
Sweden				−977	−753	−1027	−1123
United Kingdom	−1364	−2070	−1585	−5023	−2276	−1711	−5659

Source: derived from Court of Auditors annual reports.

import duties are collected at the port of entry rather than in the country where they are consumed. Thus German imports coming through Rotterdam would result in duties being collected by the Netherlands which would pay them into the budget. Similarly, payments for the removal of agricultural surpluses may be made in countries other than those of the producing farmers. In addition to these budgetary considerations, there are also real **resource transfers** because consumers in one member state may be paying higher than world prices for food imported from other members.

• Environmental costs
In the past, high cereal prices persuaded farmers to plough much of the chalk downs, which at world prices would have remained in traditional grazing. So ancient grasslands rich in wildlife – flowers, butterflies, birds etc. – became cornfields whose production added to cereal surpluses. This is but one illustration of an extensive catalogue of unnecessary environmental degradation caused by the CAP's past high price regime. Unfortunately it is very difficult to recapture lost habitats, and impossible to recreate lost species, so the reformed CAP does not represent a return to paradise lost.

Summary
How much the CAP has cost the UK is unknown. The four costs identified are of three types. The simplest is that of budgetary transfers which are known. More difficult are the costs of trade diversion and resource misallocation, which can only be estimated in relation to various assumptions. A further degree of difficulty is associated with estimating environmental costs – how can you value wild flowers, butterflies or a beautiful view? Politicians usually ignore all but the budgetary costs of the CAP, and take decisions related only to these.

Other environmental benefits
Environmental 'goods' and 'bads' are difficult to estimate, but they are very important to our welfare. On many of these issues common action is essential because action by individual nations is unlikely. Acid rain is a good example. Its major source is coal-burning electricity power stations. Coal always contains some sulphur. When it is burnt, sulphurous gases enter the atmosphere appearing later in acid rain which corrodes public buildings (especially those built of limestone), acidifies lakes causing the death of fish, and harms large areas of pine forest in northern Europe. Removing sulphurous gases from power station smoke is expensive, and so increases the costs of gener-

ating electricity. No government will want to see its costs rise by unilaterally introducing desulphurization. The Conservative regimes of 1981 to 1997 were markedly reluctant to undertake environmental projects. The fact that in the first half of the 1990s the UK introduced its first power station desulphurization plant and began cleaning up its drinking water and its beaches was due to EU rather than UK policy.

Conclusion: is membership of the EU a good thing?

At the time of writing, December 2000, the UK has been a member for twenty-seven years. Has membership been of net economic benefit so far and what of the future? Looking at the past, a conclusion is surprisingly difficult. The most widely acknowledged consequence of membership was the high budgetary costs to the UK of the CAP in the 1970s and early 1980s. Other costs and benefits are difficult to estimate. One pointer, already mentioned above, is that prior to membership the UK's GDP was growing much more slowly than the average for the Community, but has fared better since accession. Unfortunately such information is capable of very different interpretations; it might be argued, for example, that outside the Community the UK's relative economic decline could have been reversed more effectively. No definitive answer to these questions seems possible. Indeed, no study of the economics of membership has produced any clear answer to these questions.

Of course the reasons for the UK being a member of the EU are not purely economic. The original motivation for a common market, discussed in Chapter 1, was the desire to cooperate economically, and politically, to prevent European wars like those of 1914-18 and 1939-45. In the EU, the former protagonists have come together in such a way as to make further wars between them unthinkable. The exercise of national sovereignty in the past lead to these wars, *sharing sovereignty* has seen an end to such wars. In the author's personal opinion, it is sad that some of the UK's current politicians ignore these facts and still appeal to nationalism in their attempts to gain power.

KEY WORDS

Sovereignty	Support costs
GDP per head	Resource transfers
Resource misallocation	Environmental degradation
Trade diversion	Environmental benefits

Further reading
Bamford, C. Chapter 13 in *Economics for AS*. CUP, 2000.
Grant, S. and Vidler, C. Part 2, Unit 25 in *Economics in Context*. Heinemann Educational, 2000.
Romer, S. Chapter 1 in *Understanding the European Union*. Anforme, 2000.

Useful website
Association for the Monetary Union of Europe; www.amue.org

Essay topics
1. (a) How can the principle of comparative advantage be used to explain some of the benefits the United Kingdom has derived from its membership of the European Union.   [12 marks]
   (b) Discuss the view that, despite these benefits, membership of the European Union is damaging the performance of the United Kingdom economy.   [13 marks]
   [AEB, Paper 2, Q10, Summer 1997.]
2. (a) Examine the costs and benefits for firms and consumers of a country being part of a free trade area.   [60 marks]
   (b) What might be the economic advantages and disadvantages for a member of the European Union which does not join the European Monetary Union?   [40 marks]
   [Edexcel, Paper 2, Q6, June 1998.]

Data response question

Section A
Answer this question.

Unilever's preparation for EMU

By January 1999, 11 European countries will have entered into a monetary union. Few companies will be as prepared for its arrival as Unilever, the Anglo-Dutch consumer group which operates in every country in the single currency zone and which makes products as diverse as ice cream, tea, margarine, Calvin Klein fragrances, Elizabeth Arden cosmetics and Persil soap powder.

The significance of the euro lies not so much in the creation of a single currency as in the contribution it will make to a much bigger process – the completion of the European Union's single market.

By removing one uncertainty in doing business across borders inside the single currency zone, the euro will allow groups such as Unilever to develop further on a European scale.

The savings from the single currency, however, will be surprisingly modest for large companies such as Unilever. Jan Naars, Unilever's group treasurer, estimates the reduction in transaction costs at no more than £20 million a year – on European turnover last year of £13.6 billion. 'The benefit will be much greater for smaller companies for whom the transaction costs are higher in proportion to sales,' he says. 'We already operate in more than 100 countries and will still have to deal with almost as many currencies.'

Unilever will start pricing in euros for transactions between its European subsidiaries from 1 January 1999 and for internal reporting from 1 January 2000, but will not make an early move towards EU-wide prices for consumers. Hans Eggerstedt, Unilever's German finance director, expects the euro to increase the pressure for price harmonization – it will be easier for consumers to spot the variations inside the monetary union. However, large organizations like Unilever are already comparing prices and buying supplies on an EU-wide scale.

The single currency will also affect the allocation of resources within the single market. 'The UK will be an unpredictable currency area for the rest of Europe,' says Mr Eggerstedt, 'despite its advantages as a manufacturing centre. We already have to deal with the consumer, the competition and the authorities – so we like to eliminate other uncertainties.'

Source: 'One more step to the single market', *Financial Times*, 4 June 1998 (adapted).

(a) Briefly explain what is meant by the following terms:
    (i) monetary union (line 2);   [2 marks]
    (ii) the single market (lines 9–10);   [2 marks]
(b) State and explain **one** way in which the euro is significant for 'the completion of the European Union's single market' (lines 9–10).
    [2 marks]
(c) (i) What is meant by 'transaction costs'? (line 19)   [1 mark]
    (ii) Why are the benefits of reductions in transaction costs 'greater for smaller companies'? (line 19)   [2 marks]

(iii) Explain **another** reason why some companies may benefit more than others from the European single currency.
[2 marks]

(d) 'The UK will be an unpredictable currency area for the rest of Europe, despite its advantages as a manufacturing centre' (lines 33–35).

(i) Explain why the UK might have 'advantages as a manufacturing centre'. [3 marks]

(ii) To what extent might the UK economy be disadvantaged by the decision to delay entry into the Economic and Monetary Union? [6 marks]

[OCR, Economics of Europe paper, Q1, March 2000.]

Conclusion

All for one and one for all (Dumas)

When one now observes the progress of economic and political integration in the European Union, it is difficult to believe that just over 55 years ago most of its members were in the depths of the Second World War. That war involved the four largest EU members as some of the main antagonists, two on one side, two on the other. It was separated from a similar preceding war by only one generation. If the coming together in the European Union of these previously warring factions had no other effect than to prevent a further war, the Union would be a great economic success, for even ignoring the terrible human costs, the economic waste of those two wars was enormous. The prevention of war seems a rather negative benefit; this chapter now looks at the positive side where *all for one and one for all* is becoming literally true through the process of economic integration. We must look at the economic progress which has been achieved and the prospects for further progress in a Europe of rapid and accelerating change.

The economic success of the Community

During the 1960-90 period the economies of the fifteen grew more rapidly than that of the USA. As Table 21 shows, in 1960 the GDP per head in the USA was 80 per cent higher than that in the EU, but by 1990 the American lead was reduced to about 37 per cent. Over the same period Japanese GDP per head rocketed from being about 57 per

Table 21 GDP per head: EUR15 compared with USA and Japan, 1960–2000 (EUR15 = 100)

	USA	Japan
1960	162.2	56.8
1970	145.6	90.4
1980	140.9	97.1
1990	137.3	113.0
1995	146.6	115.0
2000 (forecast)	150.8	109.8

The comparison is in terms of purchasing power parity.

Source: *European Economy 69,* 1999.

cent of that in the EU to gaining a lead of nearly 13 per cent. During the 1990s, the USA increased its lead over the EU, but Japan's lead was reduced. The report on European relative economic progress must be 'fairly good but could do better!'

Economic growth has been very variable during the Community's first four decades. Table 22 shows that initially growth was rapid, but worldwide recessions, largely caused by oil price shocks in 1974 and again in 1979, greatly reduced growth, and led to the under-employment of resources in general and labour in particular. After 1984 growth began to accelerate but unemployment, although falling, remained high compared to the 1960s. The improvements in the 1980s can be attributed to three main factors:

- success in controlling inflation
- the implementation of supply-side policies
- the introduction of the single market.

As noted in Chapter 3 there are still some NTBs, notably differences in certain tax rates and excise duties, distorting competition and hindering the operation of comparative advantage. But these factors are not sufficient to explain the slowdown in the first half of the 1990s – economic growth slowed, and unemployment increased.

The Commission blamed an undeserved loss of confidence. Within Europe the 1990 German reunification was far more expensive than expected, and simultaneously the recession in the UK rapidly deep-

Table 22 EUR15 – some economic indicators 1961–2000

	1961 –73	1974 –85	1986 –90	1991 –95	1996	1997	1998	1999	2000 (fore-cast)
Growth of GDP (real annual %)	4.8	2.0	3.2	1.5	1.6	2.5	2.6	2.1	3.0
Gross capital formation (as % GDP)	25.6	22.8	21.8	20.7	19.7	19.8	20.4	20.7	21.2
Labour productivity growth rate (%)	4.4	2.0	1.8	2.1	1.3	1.7	1.3	0.9	1.8
Employment change (annual %)	0.3	0.1	1.5	-0.5	0.5	0.8	1.4	1.4	1.3
Unemployment (%)	2.3	6.4	8.8	10.0	9.4	10.9	9.9	9.2	8.6
Government debt (% of GDP)	-	53.0	54.5	71.6	69.6	71.6	70.6	68.6	67.5
Inflation rate GDP deflator	5.2	10.6	5.0	3.8	2.5	1.9	2.0	1.5	1.8

Source: *European Economy 69,* 1999.

ened. It is probable that such problems in two of the largest economies of the Union were significant factors in the slowdown, and affected all. Also significant, was the raising of German interest rates to counter the inflationary costs of re-unification. These higher interest rates forced the interest rates of other countries higher at a time when slowing economies required lower rates. France pleaded with Germany to reduce rates, but to no avail; Germany gives the prevention of inflation a high priority. In the latter half of the 1990s there was some recovery, with economic growth accelerating, and government debt, inflation and unemployment falling.

Appraisal of EU economic strategy

Since the early days of the Community, the Commission has been formulating long-term plans. The boxed article about the Stockholm IGC provides a recent example of the EU's planning horizon. This is in marked contrast to the UK government attitude prevalent from

---

STOCKHOLM EUROPEAN COUNCIL 23 AND 24 MARCH 2001

This was the first Annual Spring Meeting on economic and social questions. In future the European Council will use these annual meetings to focus on this policy area.

EU objective for the next decade: *to become the most competitive and dynamic knowledge-based economy in the world, capable of sustainable economic growth with more and better jobs and greater social cohesion.*

Priority is to be given to achieving full employment in a competitive economy. To achieve this the Council discussed common policy actions:

* to create more and better jobs,
* to accelerate economic reform,
* to modernise the European social model,
* to harness new technologies.

Solving the following problems was highlighted as being essential to progress:

* an ageing population of which people of working age constitute an ever smaller part,
* the need for economic policy to provide stable macroeconomic conditions in order to achieve sustained growth,
* the candidate countries should be actively involved in the goals and procedures to achieve these objectives.

1979 to 1997; here, investment decisions have been regarded as the sole prerogative of firms and businesses operating in a free market. The 1998 EU budget provided about 3.5bn Ecu (about £2.3bn) for research and development, concentrated particularly on high-technology areas. Is such public intervention in research more effective (in terms of economic growth) than leaving it to industry? The experiences of Japan and the USA provide some pointers. Japanese leadership in many areas of technology has resulted from many years of public intervention, with huge expenditures being targeted on correctly identified growth areas. Post-Second World War high growth rates in the USA have been attributed to civil spin-offs from gigantic military research programmes, for example, the original Boeing airliner, the first major successful jet airliner, came from a very expensively developed military aircraft. The slower USA growth rate of the 1980s correlates with the rapid reduction of military research expenditures – suggesting that the market alone is not the best deliverer of economic growth even in the most capitalistic of cultures.

The more rapid growth of the USA compared to the EU over the last decade is attributable partly to the differential effects of globalisation on their economies. As discussed in Chapter 7 high labour mobility, due largely to a low level of social security in the USA, has lead to lower job security and hence wages, but much higher employment. In sharp contrast, generous social security in the EU results in labour market rigidities, higher wages but lower employment. The EU acknowledges that unemployment is its major problem. Its attempts to reduce it through improved education and training seem to be working, but work motivation is bound to be less than in the USA where incentives are more brutal. As in other areas of economics, there is a clear trade-off between equity and efficiency.

Welfare
It is a truism that money cannot buy happiness. Neither can GDP per head fully measure economic welfare. GDP excludes many things which we tend to take for granted but which are important to our well being – peace, security, plentiful food supplies, freedom and democracy. There is little doubt that in an uncertain world the size and strength of the EU more effectively protects these matters, which are fundamental to our welfare, than individual nations acting separately. Perhaps this is the real reason why both prosperous and poor countries continue to be attracted to the EU.

Conclusion

The European Union has developed from its original six members to nine, to ten, to twelve, to fifteen and still more countries wish to join. Clearly in the eyes of many the Union is a success. The continuing development of the single market promises to further enhance the Union's economy – already it is the world's largest developed country market in terms of population and as Adam Smith observed, 'specialization is limited by the extent of the market' – meaning that efficiency depends on market size. The Community has the potential to become, within a generation, the world's major economic power.

The EU attempts to further the process of making *all into one* by emphasising political integration as well as economic integration. Indeed the former is essential to the progress of economic and monetary union. But there is a conflict between this deepening of the current Union and its widening to include the much poorer CEECs. Reconciling these conflicts will be the major challenge of the next decade and beyond.

Index